REACHABLE
MOMENTS

REACHABLE MOMENTS

A Unique Perspective from
The Desk of a Teacher

By Randy Sexton

DEDICATED TO

My wife, Jackie, who supported and encouraged me throughout the writing process.

To the many students whose lives I became a small part of during my years as a teacher.

ACKNOWLEDGEMENTS

I have many people to thank for making happen my *Reachable Moments*. I began writing memoirs for the book in June 2006, jotting down a few summaries and philosophical musings about my life as a middle school teacher. I began to jot down things that happened during my career just so I could remember them later. My mom, Ruby Lee Layson, who was a far better writer than I will ever be, would read what I had written, help with editing and share her feedback. She was the most influential person regarding my lifetime of writing. I wish she could still be here today to read my narratives and to share in my enthusiasm for finally publishing them.

My wife, Jackie, would usually be the first one to see the first drafts of my writings. First drafts sometimes were not my best effort, but Jackie would read whatever I gave her, and she was kind enough to share her thoughts. Sometimes I would return to my computer to edit my work with my spirits a bit crushed. I think she made me a better writer because I valued her approval as I would present each new piece of writing. Jackie also sat alone downstairs as I pounded away on the computer keyboard. She was patient with me, and I thank her for that.

Heather Hardin was one of the teachers with whom I worked very closely at the middle school. Heather would look at what I had written and was always very encouraging. She helped me with the editing and together we would reflect on the many adventures we had shared with the students in our years of working side-by-side. Our conversations have inspired me to realize that there are still many more stories to tell.

Rebecca Radcliff was one of our students, and she always had complete confidence that my writing would be published. Rebecca was not like any student I had ever worked with before. She was a brilliant young lady who suffered all the anxieties of being twelve, and thirteen, and fourteen while in middle school, but who also had the intellect of any well-educated adult I had ever met. She read many of my early pieces and helped me believe that I was a writer. Rebecca is one of the few students that I stay in touch with and regard, now, as a friend.

I cannot say enough about author George Fleming and his influence on my writing. I met George and his wife, Linda, a few years ago, in a salsa club in Cartagena, Columbia. George had recently published the first of his Tampa Bay Tropics Thrillers, *Bad Habits*, and was on the same Carnival cruise as Jackie and me. We were destined for the Panama Canal, but our stop in Cartagena was a comedy of errors that ended up with the four of us being left in the salsa club while the other forty-six people from our bus were taken to the next scheduled event on the tour. To paraphrase Humphrey Bogart in *Casablanca, this was the beginning of a beautiful friendship.*

George has advised me on each piece of writing in this book. He has encouraged me, criticized me, and been honest with me about my writing and how to go through the steps of writing, revising, editing, and publishing. George is now a good personal friend and his four *Tampa Bay Tropics* Thrillers have kept me on the edge of my seat for hours. You can find George's books on Amazon.

While I'm at it, I should thank a few more writers, some living, and others long gone. I am thankful to my University of Kentucky teachers who taught me about writers like Twain, Steinbeck, Hemingway, and Faulkner. I studied all those writers in college, and one might recognize their influence on how I imitated their narration or borrowed a character's name here and there. Kentucky writers Gurney Norman and Ed McClanahan were two of my college teachers. Both published their own books, too. They won't remember me, but such is the fate of all teachers to influence others and never know it.

There have been many other people and events in my life that influenced my desire to be a writer, and I apologize for not mentioning them all. John Abramson, Larry Basham, and David Reber (rest in peace, my friends) put me through various life experiences that influenced what I wrote about. Students from the middle school where I spent most of my career and from the Jack Weaver School in Southern California inspired me with (mostly) true stories that could only have been told because of them.

I have wanted to be a writer for most of my life. Unfortunately, the financial risk is so uncertain that at best it is only an obsession or a hobby while life deals out the cards. Writing isn't really something one does because he or she hopes to become rich and famous. Most who hope to get published probably share with me that sensation that there is something pulsing from inside, bursting to get out. Writers have a need to open that blood-filled artery and let the contents explode all over the empty page.

I have always felt that if I could share some of my life events, others would agree with me that I do have something to contribute, something worth reading. That may be vanity, but these events are what make us who we are. Each of us is unique because of what we have experienced and with whom we have experienced it. We may find that we have a lot in common with other people, but it is important to realize that there is no one who is just like any of us!

This is what makes life worth living and makes every day on this earth so amazing.

In the way I have written it, this book could not have been written by anybody else. It is my unique perspective. It took all the people I have mentioned above and all the events of my life to write it. I have opened myself up and I invite you to step inside and have a look around. I hope my offerings bring you joy, smiles, and a thoughtful perspective on what it means to be a teacher and mentor to young people.

CONTENTS

DRIVEN TO TEACH

When I first began interviewing for teaching jobs, I used to worry about the interviewer who would ask that inevitable question: "What is your philosophy of education?"

I thought, to answer that question, I'd have to write a book! And I did! I spent the summer of 2007 working on a book that was mainly for teachers to read, and in it, I wrote about my own teaching experiences working with a variety of kids. I also shared my p*hilosophy of education* through the narratives I wrote. The incomplete book sat in a folder, unpublished and gathering dust, until very recently. It has certainly helped me gain some perspective on my own educational philosophies and made me reflect on what kind of teacher I wanted to be.

When I enrolled at the University of Kentucky, I didn't realize it was so I would become a teacher. Like many of my peers, I didn't know what I wanted to do. I liked to read, and I loved going to stage productions and movies. I criticized my friends who used their own language incorrectly, and I cringed when I heard them use expressions like, "I'm not for sure" and "of a morning" or "I dun did that already!" There was a sleeping teacher inside me, but I didn't realize it.

Meanwhile, I was finding work in jobs with young people at group homes and mental hospitals. I was helping kids whose lives had taken a bad turn. I felt good about this, as I sensed the impact my willingness to *just listen to what they had to say* made on their futures. But the jobs didn't pay very well. I couldn't even afford to live in a cheap apartment. I could barely afford to buy macaroni and cheese and Ramen Noodles at the grocery store. I needed a better education, and I took advantage of applying for grants and loans to get it.

After completing some of the basic college requirements, I followed a close friend into his teaching program and the wheels of my teaching career began to turn.

STUDENT TEACHER

I think that I began to realize my educational philosophy when I did my student teaching placement. I enjoyed cutting up with the kids and making the lesson fun. I also tried to be funny when I could. I often laughed and got the kids laughing with me as I was teaching. Unfortunately, the teacher with whom I had been placed was much more serious and stricter about discipline and behavior in the classroom. As a result, she didn't like the atmosphere I created. The kids did, though. They learned from my teaching method, and I was having a good time with them. I felt comforted by the ones I overheard whispering to each other, "Mr. Sexton is cool!" I began developing cooperative relationships with kids. I'm not sure, but I think I made the regular class teacher feel a little bit threatened. She probably was relieved to see me finish the placement, but it was during student teaching that I realized that I really wanted to be a teacher.

MIDDLE SCHOOL

The main reason I started out as a middle school teacher was to eventually position myself for a teaching job at the high school level. A friend helped me get the interview in Melungeon County, and I was offered a seventh-grade position working with special education kids. The part I liked best about this job was that I would be collaborating with regular education teachers and bringing my kids to their regular classes. This was called "inclusion." It was described to me as "a piece of cake" by the principal who interviewed me for the job..

However, the work was challenging. Cecil, an African American boy of 13 years, was hard-headed and street tough. He hung out with boys in the high school and was as big and intimidating as many of them. Judie was a proud redneck country girl who was equally stubborn and argued with me at every opportunity. I will never forget the time I tried to put her to work on an assignment in a class of 30 students and she turned angrily to me and shouted, with a southern twang, "You get on my nerves!" The other kids to whom I was assigned were equally hard to work with in their own way. I learned a lot in that first year.

Teaching middle school gradually became a dream job for me because I began to see that many of these kids were accepting me. They were becoming more dependent upon me. They began to appreciate my devotion to them and my desire to see them succeed where they had failed in the past. The regular education students also took an interest in getting to know me, and often asked for my help. I gave it gratefully. In a very short time, middle school became a natural fit for me.

I didn't realize it at the time, but teaching middle school grows on a teacher. While it is difficult and has many disappointments, there are few moments more exciting and enlightening than when students accept and appreciate your help!

After eight years, I was offered a position teaching regular education in Language Arts. I nervously accepted, but it was an excellent decision. I was to teach subjects that I knew well: Greek mythology, Shakespeare, poetry, American literature, and writing! I would have special education students *and* the regular education students. The seventh grade had always been challenging, but I believed my students appreciated my *philosophy of education.*

PHILOSOPHY

My philosophy of education is that there is much more to good teaching than educating students about reading and writing. Gail Godwin said, "Good teaching is one-fourth preparation and three-fourths theater." I believe it. This is why I would show up to teach Poe's "Raven" wearing a black bird on the shoulder of my shirt. This is why I created PowerPoints with dramatic pictures for Silverstein's poem, "The Winner," and used my most masculine voice to narrate it to the class. This is why I often had students come to the front of the room and act out a death scene from many of Shakespeare's plays instead of just reading their parts. This is why I tried to show up in my classroom with a smile on my face and a positive attitude toward each student. As they came into the hallway, I knew that my mood would set the tone for the rest of the day. It was important to greet them and let them know that whatever problems they may have left at home that day, they were starting fresh in this home away from home.

I believe an effective teacher must have some relationship with every student in the room. This is difficult in a middle school with about thirty of them in every class. And they came from so many different walks of life! They were decadently rich, and they were ridiculously poor. They were bathed, and they reeked from the cat pee their clothes got soiled in the last time they dropped them on the floor and put them back on the next day. They had loving families, and they were abused. They were exceptionally intelligent, and they were functionally deficient. They had been skipped a grade, and they had been held back once or even twice. They were carrying around security blankets and dolls, and they were using drugs and experimenting with sex. Every one of them wanted to walk into a classroom where the teacher wouldn't let them feel threatened, or stupid, or invisible.

Middle school students want to believe that their teacher cares about them. I loved overhearing my students announcing proudly (and simultaneously), "I'm Mr. Sexton's favorite!"

Reachable moments with these kids were not always

easy for me, but I always believed that the reach should start with a smile. There is an old expression among many teachers that goes, "You never smile until after Christmas." If you are a middle school teacher, don't believe it. My philosophy is that teachers should start with a smile which conveys the message that we have faith in them. Be patient. Let the classroom be a place where every kid is special. Treat them all fairly, but don't treat them all the same. They are all different, and there is no time in their lives that they are more aware of their differences than early adolescence.

THE PERFECT TEACHER

The lord Jesus took his disciples up on a mountainside, and he began to teach them.

"Blessed are the poor in spirit, for theirs is the kingdom of heaven."

And Matthew said, "Should I be taking notes on this stuff?"

Jesus went on, "Blessed are those who mourn, for they will be comforted. Blessed are the meek, for they will inherit the earth."

And Judas said, laughing "I'd sure like to inherit me a big piece of the earth!"

Jesus continued, "Blessed are those who hunger and thirst for righteousness. Blessed are the merciful. Blessed are the pure in heart."

And Simon Peter said, "Is there going to be a test over all of this?"

Jesus put up a finger and said, "Blessed are the peacemakers, for they will be called sons of God."

And Andrew leaned over to Bartholomew and whispered, "Hey,

Dude, can I borrow some parchment and a stylus?"

Jesus stepped closer to them all and said, "Blessed are those who are persecuted because of righteousness, for theirs is the kingdom of heaven."

And Phillip raised his hand, saying, "Can I go to the bathroom, please?"

Jesus smiled patiently at Phillip and said, "Blessed are you when people insult you and persecute you and lie about you because of me."

And John said, "Could you repeat what you said after "blessed are the poor?" My 504 modifications say you have to go slowly and check for understanding."

Then two Pharisees. who had been whispering from behind the crowd the entire time, stepped forward, grim-faced.

The first one said, "May I see your lesson plans with the Core Standards and your student engagement strategies?

The other Pharisee said, "Have you written down the Essential Questions with a learning target in a location where all of your students can see the objective before the lesson begins?"

And Jesus wept.

THE AWARD

In May of 2006, my tenth year as a Melungeon County Middle School teacher,
I was sitting in a faculty meeting. I had been told it was an important one, but I really didn't think it would be any different from every other faculty meeting I'd attended throughout the school year. Many of the other teachers in attendance knew, however.

The meeting began with the principal, Mr. Cramer, introducing the manager of the city's local Wal-Mart.

The manager, a heavy-set man about my age (late-forties), stepped forward. He said a few words about how much Wal-Mart and the community of Melungeon County appreciated the hard work of our teachers. "I know most of you," he said, "and some of you remember when I was in your classrooms. It's my pleasure to be here today as a representative of the Wal-Mart Corporation to recognize all of you as an outstanding team of teachers and to recognize one of you in particular. It's strange to me that I don't know this teacher personally. We conducted a '*students only*' vote at the store in which students voted for the teacher of the year, and this teacher's name kept coming up. Usually, students select an elementary school teacher. This year is the first time a middle school teacher has won the award."

He paused and looked around the room, as if searching. All of us were silent.

"The Teacher of the Year for 2006 is Randy Sexton."

As you might imagine, I was so stunned I sat there for a moment not comprehending and not sure how to react. The teachers, administrators, office staff, and others who were present for this meeting had burst into a spontaneous applause. I was oblivious to that as well.

Mrs. Johansson, a Language Arts teacher, and close friend, was seated beside me. She nudged me with her elbow to bring me back from my daze and let me know that I needed to get up and accept this honor.

I stood amid all the smiling faces and enthusiastic applause, and slowly walked up to the manager. He shook my hand and gave me a plaque that said, *Wal-Mart Teacher of the Year 2006 Presented to Randy Sexton, Melungeon County Middle School.* He also gave me a shirt with a similar declaration and a thousand-dollar check which I could spend on the school however I wished.

Still in a fog, I turned to the others in the room. They were now standing and cheering for me loudly. The librarian, Mrs. Milam, directed me to turn toward her and hold up the plaque as she snapped photos. I smiled, dimly aware of what was happening.

I was overwhelmed with confusion. How had I been selected for this honor? I was in a room with many outstanding teachers, and there were many more throughout the county. I was being recognized for a job that I knew I had done well, but I have always been almost painfully aware that I am nothing like *The Perfect Teacher.* Secretly, I have always believed that I was not fully competent. I had looked at many of the other teachers in amazement so many times. All were devoted to their students and their subject. They really knew their stuff. I realized this individual award was only because of all the support I had received from the teams of teachers with whom I had been working. *It takes a village,* after all.

A teaching job is different from any other job I have ever known. It isn't a competition. It is dependent upon a team of teachers who lift you up and make you better. It is all about teachable, reachable moments with students, because the better the connection a teacher has with his or her students, the more willingly they will listen to what is being taught.

I returned to my seat, receiving a series of thumps on the back and congratulatory handshakes. Mrs. Johansson smiled broadly and grasped my arm. "Congratulations, Randy!"

She admitted that she and many of the other teachers knew that I would be receiving the award.

Mr. Cramer brought the meeting to order, reviewing concerns about the final days of the school year and what we were to do today in our department meetings.

I heard almost nothing he said.

If I'm being honest, this award felt amazing. It was the pinnacle of my years as a teacher. I felt the surge of many emotions. The honor was a crowning event that turned years of working with many difficult students into a feeling of success and smiles.

I was unable to discipline a student for the rest of the year, however, because every time I would start to do so, the student and other students around them would have some sweet comment, letting me know I was appreciated.

As I marched my class down the hallway to lunch, I would say, "Get your line single-file and quiet!" and a student would chirp, "We love you, Mr. Sexton!" Cheers of agreement would echo in the hallway as I put my finger to my mouth to *shush* them, but it was almost pointless.

The smile in my eyes (which were always puffy, dark, and swollen by these last few weeks of the school year) gave away too much information. And I loved them too.

As a middle school teacher, I know that I have done many things wrong over the years. I hope I have also done some things right, too. You don't always know right away.

My Teacher of the Year award wasn't really for the 2006 year, but for all the years leading up to 2006. It was the result of the votes of students who had been in my classroom since I began teaching in Melungeon County, Kentucky, about a decade earlier. As I said, I believe I have done some things right. I have been re-membered fondly by students who have come through my door over the years. I have formed lasting relation-ships with some of them, perhaps taught them a little something as they passed through, and even accepted friend requests from them on Facebook or Instagram once their middle school internment was over.

A teacher is different from a parent, and different from a friend. A teacher experiences everything with his or her students from a unique perspective. If the teacher pays attention, he or she can be an important piece on the chessboard of a student's life.

Teachers often don't realize how important they were until many years later. More often, they will never know at all. This influence can be good for the student, or it can be bad. There is a lot on the line for a teacher who works with the multiple personalities that walk into a classroom.

After my 2006 year, I began to stash away my lesson plans, teaching materials, letters from students, and things I hoped to continue to use in the coming years. I wondered if I might, someday, write a book of short stories about these things as my career was coming to an end. It might not sell very well, but it would come from a unique perspective. Perhaps it would be a book that could help new teachers and give some ideas to old ones. It might be worth a read for parents, teachers, and students if I could find a clever way to share my experiences and responses to different situations.

I often wondered how I could make a difference in the world, with all the anger, pain, division, and hatred that has revealed itself of late. It's better to do something small than to do nothing at all. So, I decided to write these stories, and share my thoughts. The first steps in publishing my work are the offerings I have collected here: short, mostly true narratives of my own experiences with the multiple personalities that have been in my classroom. In most cases, I changed the names of the students in each story. Melungeon County is also a fictitious location, and I may have "stretched the truth" a bit for reasons of personal confidentiality.

This is hardly the definitive book on how to work with adolescent children. I have stepped into a few potholes in my dealings with adolescents, but the successes outweigh the burden of the failures. I have had some fascinating experiences, and I have witnessed events that were funny, or sad, or relatable to anyone who has experienced the drama of dealing with a pre-teen or teenager.

The following pages have poured out from my heart and were guided by my muse, who I hope has directed my hands to write of inspirations, sorrows, and successes in the lives of young people, and the unique joys of teaching these amazing and unique human beings.

FIFTH PERIOD OR: HOW I LEARNED TO STOP WORRYING AND LOVE MY STUDENTS

My planning period was about to end. My fourth period Language Arts class would be coming back from lunch and through my classroom door very soon. I had a few minutes before the bell would ring, so I thought it was a good time to go over to my old Captain's Chair and get on the computer to check my school email.

The principal and other teachers often communicated through this medium, but I would have to be quick so I could rush out into the hallways and redirect students as they meandered to their next classes.

Almost mechanically, I moved to my chair and collapsed into it.

It was then that I felt the hard metal of the torn arm rest as it bit into the back, right pocket of my dress pants. I groaned aloud, not from pain, but from the realization that I had torn my pants… again.

I felt rather foolish because this wasn't the first time this had happened. Less than six weeks ago I had torn my pants on the same, jagged armrest, only that time it happened at the end of the school day, and the tear had been much smaller. The only place I had to be visible then was during my after-school bus duty, and I could wear my jacket so nobody would see the rip.

This was different.

The rip in my pants was about four inches long, and

then it took a very sharp turn for another three inches across. The tear hung like a flap at the entrance to a tent. Fortunately, a white pocket blocked out what might have been a traumatizing view for many middle school students. The pants were black, the pocket, white. This would be noticed as soon as I began walking around in my classroom.

Thinking quickly, I abandoned my first thought to remove the pants quickly and staple the flap back to the tear-- not enough time, and it would still look bad.

Seconds remained until the bell!

What to do?

I found the clear tape dispenser sitting on my desk. I pulled some four to five-inch-long strips from it. I gently applied the tape to strategic locations along the backside of my pants.

The tape held!

I examined the angle of the tape and concluded that it would last until I could go home at the end of the day. The pants would have to be discarded because they were beyond repair, but I could make them work for now.

The bell rang, and I went into the hallway just outside my classroom door. Self-consciously, my back against the wall, I watched the students run, dance, and wander into the hall, oblivious to my situation. In minutes, my classroom was full of marauding seventh graders.

"Everyone please get seated and quiet," I commanded, putting the torn pants out of my mind, and getting on to the business of the day's lesson. "Today we're going to talk about an American writer named Samuel

Clemons. You might recognize him by a different name. Do any of you remember a vocabulary word we were learning about last week? It was *pseudonym*. What does that word mean? *Pseudonym?*"

Immediately, three or four hands went up. Other students looked at me expectantly, confident that if I did pick them, they would give the correct answer. This was my accelerated class, and all of them were smarter than I, even if they didn't yet know as much. I took the student who was fastest on the draw. "Elle?"

(Her name was pronounced "L")

Elle looked at me with great wisdom on her perfectly freckled face and said, "Mr. Sexton, did you know you have tape on your pants?"

"Yes, Elle," I confessed, blushing. "Thank you."

I noticed that the rest of the class had begun to examine my derriere.

"I tore my pants on the armrest of my chair and was trying to keep it from being too noticeable," I sighed, letting the sound out a little too loudly, like a semi-truck locking its brakes.

I was trying to be honest, hoping the students wouldn't be too hard on me.

Glancing around the room as I explained, the amused looks on the faces of my students seemed to say, *Oh, you poor idiot!*

And that was the end of it.

I went on with the lesson somewhat self-consciously but made it through without further comment.

… Until the next bell rang.

My fifth period class came into the room as I was

sitting at my computer, checking attendance on Infinite Campus, the latest technology in the keeping of records. As I stood up and started walking around my desk to repeat my lesson for a fourth time, I was interrupted by Corey, who had never quite caught on to the *raise your hand before speaking* rule. This was my own fault because it was a rarely enforced rule in my classroom.

"Hey, Mr. Sexton," he said. "Did you know you have tape on your butt?"

A couple of students craned their heads to get a better look.

"I wondered what that was," announced Megan.

"Oh, yeah," said Sarah, who always sat beside Megan, "I saw that too but wasn't going to say anything."

Other students took on the same amused look as the last class.

"Yes," I responded with a self-deprecating laugh. "I tore my pants on the arm rest of my chair. Check out that jagged metal sticking out of it!" I motioned to the chair from which I had risen. "See how the rubber piece has torn off?"

Was I pleading? Was I excusing my clumsiness? Probably.

"I put the tape on to hold the pants together until I get home."

I grinned at them uncomfortably.

Suddenly, I noticed that I had the attention of the entire class! It seemed that everyone was listening! Isn't that what a teacher is supposed to do?

"I guess tape isn't very good solution, is it?"

Over in their usual corner of the room, Cassie, Sara, and Christa (whose older brother, Paul, had always asked me to mention his name if I ever got anything published) huddled with their heads together and then let out a simultaneous giggle. Early in the school year I had started calling the three of them *Charlie's Angels* (I, of course, was Charlie. We four would walk through the halls of the seventh grade with our fingers pretending to be guns! But I digress.) and this incident was just another in the list of anecdotes they might one day tell their children.

Suddenly, Megan stood up from her desk.

"Well," she said, "this might help."

Megan picked up my tape dispenser and pulled several strips of tape from it. Then she applied the tape to the back pocket of her jeans.

"We can say it's a fashion statement!" she announced, handing the dispenser to Sarah, who passed it next to Corey, who passed it on to the student next to him.

Several students put the tape on their own pants and then sat back down.

The angels rushed over to the tape dispenser and tore off several strips for themselves. Other students in the classroom did the same. In all, fifteen or sixteen students would walk out of my classroom with tape on their pants.

"Wow" I said, "Thanks!"

I began the lesson, and it wasn't more than a few minutes before Ryan, sitting near the back of the room, raised his hand.

"Hey, Mr. Sexton! Did you know you got tape on

the back of your pants?"

There's always one who is playing in a field of butterflies.

"Yes, Ryan, it's a fashion statement," I declared. "People used to wear their pants backward, or sag their pants, but the cool thing now it to put tape on them."

Ryan looked puzzled.

"Megan, would you show him what I'm talking about?"

Megan stood up and turned around so Ryan could see the tape on her pants. I called to other students who had done the same.

"Courtney? Dakota? Stephen?"

Each of them stood and turned to show the class their taped pants pocket. Students who had not been in on the game but had been following the action were giggling. I smiled in appreciation of my seventh graders' unique solution to the problem.

I made it through the rest of the day with a child-like grin. Each time someone pointed out the tear in my pants, and the tape I was using, I told them the tape was a new trend, and if they wanted to, they could take some from my dispenser. To be honest, there were not many takers, but the mood had been made lighter by this turn of events. It was a *reachable moment* I would not soon forget and reminded me why it was so easy to love my students.

Years later, a professor for one of my master's level college classes would give me a writing assignment asking, "Why Are You Driven to Teach Middle School?" I wrote an articulate enough response and submitted it.

Looking back, though, I wish I had simply given him this memoir.

A LESSON FOR THE TEACHER

The use of technology for classroom instruction is something school administrators encourage when they are examining the lesson plans submitted by classroom teachers. I have never been much good with technology, but I had come up with an idea to implement the use of a *Smartboard* in one of my lessons. A *Smartboard* is an interactive projection display that projects a computer's video output. In other words, it's a fancy overhead projector.

I was quite proud of the idea I had come up with because it also involved allowing an individual student an opportunity to help teach the lesson. Getting student involvement was yet another activity that administrators liked to see in a lesson plan. Most of the activities I preferred to do in my classroom naturally got the students involved, but this lesson would be submitted to my department head in a written format which explained *how* I was going to do it.

School administrators gobbled that crap up.

Sheldon Saponi was one of the brightest students in the seventh grade. Maybe he was one of the brightest ever to come through my classroom door. He loved history and seemed to be a bottomless pit of knowledge about World War II. He attended mostly accelerated classes and some of those were occasionally interrupted by the Gifted and Talented Education teacher, who would pull him out of class for conferencing and advanced instruction.

Sheldon was not athletic during his middle school years, but he was a little taller and bigger than the average seventh grader. He had a build that could have been molded into the body of a wrestler or a nose guard on the football field. These things didn't interest him until he got into high school. For Sheldon, middle school was all about being the smartest kid in the classroom, and he was pretty good at that.

He generally got excellent grades, academically, but his wisdom and intelligence had made him a bit arrogant and condescending toward his peers, and sometimes, his teachers. While he was a very high-functioning student, his social skills were below average. He often argued with people at school, and many students found him annoying. As a result, he didn't have many close friends. The peer group that I mostly saw him hanging around with was the other socially awkward kids who would more than likely blossom into financially successful adults after their college years were over but struggled socially in middle school.

One of the pieces Sheldon had written for his portfolio that year was a myth, assigned by me. He had decided to call it *Charlimedes Brownicus*. Charlimedes was an ancestor of our (somewhat) modern *Charlie Brown*. It was brilliant. I liked it so much that I asked Sheldon if he would mind if I shared it in class as part of a Smartboard presentation. Reluctantly, he consented. It didn't occur to me that a student as brilliant as Sheldon might be sensitive to constructive criticism.

Sheldon was in my first period Literature class. Before the lesson began, I thanked him in front of the other students and praised him for writing such a clever piece. I mentioned his sense of humor for using characters from the original Charlie Brown (*Snoopius* was one, and *Lucy* was another. I suggested in front of the class that *Lucillius* might be a fun name for her, but he seemed to bristle at my suggestion). He also included the gods of Greek mythology in the story, and because they were adults, he used adult dialogue as it is used in the Charlie Brown cartoons, "*Wah Wah wah-wah wah-wah...*"

I turned on the Smartboard and Sheldon's typewritten story burst onto the screen.

"Sheldon," I started, "I really love how you began your creative writing piece. "

He let out a nervous giggle and said, "Thank you."

"If you don't mind, I thought maybe you could read the piece, and we could ask you questions as we go through it as a class. Would that be okay?"

"I guess so," Sheldon replied, tentatively.

He read the first paragraph at my request.

"The morning sun rose with Apollo over the Greek isles as the youthful Charlimedes Brownicus awoke to meet the day. He awoke with his tame Chimaera, Snoopius, who was laying

on a tall boulder. "Good morning, Snoopius," he said. "I'm off to Athens for the festival of Athena today. You stay here and guard the house. And please don't set it on fire like you did the last time I left you at home unsupervised. Charlimedes was a young man, roughly the age to be on his own, but still capable of traveling great distances such as the town of Athens and other faraway lands."

When he concluded his introductory paragraph, I stopped him and said, "Very nice, Sheldon! Does anybody want to make a comment about that first paragraph?"

Becca, who counted herself among Sheldon's closer friends, raised her hand. "I love how you took the names of characters from the Charlie Brown cartoons and changed them, so they sound like Greek names."

"Thanks," Sheldon smiled a thin smile and went on, "I thought it would be kind of funny to take Charlie Brown and put him in ancient Greece.

I jumped in and added, "I thought it was brilliant. I also liked that you took a mythological character, the Chimaera, or Snoopius, and warned him not to set the house on fire." I turned my attention to the students who were in the classroom, "Do you remember that we discussed the Chimaera a few weeks ago? It's a monster that can breathe fire and was slain by one of the heroes of mythology, Bellerophon."

A few students acknowledged that we had studied the Chimaera.

"One small criticism, Sheldon: I think maybe you could start a second paragraph with the last sentence, that begins, *Charlimedes was a young man...",* That way, you could give us a little more information about who he is, maybe, make us actually visualize Charlimedes."

I had barely gotten out my last word when Sheldon spoke up loudly and said, "Well, I was thinking about doing that, but this is just a first draft, and I wasn't sure what to say about him."

It was an awkward interruption, but I could see he was a little uncomfortable. I encouraged him to go ahead with the next part of his story.

"Upon arriving at the Athenian festival, the young Charlimedes quickly became intoxicated. Wandering in the city, he accidentally knocked over a fine marble bust of Athena, shattering it on the ground. Athena was enraged, but because she was a benevolent goddess, she gave him a command to make up for his offense.

"Wah Wah Wah, wah-wah, wah, wah WAH!" she said, which, translated from the tongue of the gods, meant, "As punishment for what you have done, you must retrieve my pet owl from the temple of Ares, in Sparta. If you fail, you will burn in the fires of Hades!"

"Nice job, Sheldon," I said. "You referenced the owl, which is the bird of Athena, and you also mention another god, Ares. I really think you did a good job with that. I also like how you make the language of the gods like the language of adults in the Charlie Brown cartoons---" I turned back to the class and said, "Did any of you pick up on that?"

A student in the back of the room asked timidly, "Who is Charlie Brown?"

I gave a quick explanation and asked Sheldon to continue.

"Charlimedes traveled through months of harsh weather and dangerous roads, but he made it to the Temple of Ares, in Sparta. Here, he prayed aloud, "Oh, mighty Ares, God of War, will you kindly allow me to complete a quest bestowed upon me by your half-sister, Athena? She sends me here to return her sacred owl."

"Ares agreed to grant the request, but only if Charlimedes would travel to the underworld and steal Hades' Helmet of Invisibility for his purposes of war. Now Charlimedes had a second quest to fulfil.

Charlimedes traveled all the way through the tributaries of the River Styx and into the underworld. "Oh, great Hades," he began, "Forsaker of the Dead, Keeper of Souls, will you grant me your helmet for the use of your brother, Ares, who will repay you with many fallen warriors to serve in your kingdom."

"Hades replied, "You intrigue me, young Charlimedes. I will grant your wish, but only if you can retrieve my dog, Tiberius, from the evil oracle, Lucy. Bring him back to me, and you may take my helmet."

I interrupted Sheldon's reading again, saying, "That's really some great writing! You mention Ares, God of War, then Hades, Ruler of the Underworld. I like how you mention the River Styx, which leads to the underworld. One thing that you got wrong, here is the dog's name. Hades' dog is named Cerberus, not Tiberius. You could fix that when it's time to edit our writing.

Sheldon looked at me, and for a moment I thought he looked angry. He didn't respond because a few other students made comments and had questions about where he had gotten his ideas for the story. Then he went on reading.

"Charlimedes traveled many days and nights and finally reached the oracle named Lucy. Lucy was no ordinary oracle, for she possessed no SOUL! He quickly presented his case as masterfully as he had for Ares and for Hades, and as he spoke, he carefully avoided her gaze, for common folklore had said that the gaze of Lucy could turn a man to stone. Lucy said, "If you want Tiberius back for Hades, you must do something for me. Go to the land of King Minos and have him use his magic touch to turn a boulder into gold. Bring me back the boulder, and I will give you Tiberius."

At this point in Sheldon's telling of the story, Lisa, a shy, tiny seventh grader who always sat in the back of the classroom, but always listened carefully, raised her hand. I stopped Sheldon and let him know that Lisa had a question.

"Sheldon," she said, "I think Lucy should be a gorgon, not an oracle. You said she could turn Charlimedes into stone. That's what a gorgon does."

"Ahh, good point!" I concurred. I elected not to mention King **MIDAS** right now.

Precisely as I was saying this, Sheldon replied to her angrily, "Yeah, well it's MY story!"

I watched the confidence fade from Lisa's face.

She looked down at her desk. In the slightly darkened room, I could see that Sheldon's face had flushed red.

"Sheldon," my voice was even, but I believed he could hear the cautioning tone I hoped for, "All students are invited to give helpful criticism as we go over the story today. You need to hear what they have to say, and then decide for yourself if this is a change you want to make. Don't be rude."

"I'm sorry," he glanced at me, then to Lisa, "I'm sorry!"

"Would you like to read the rest of the story?"

"Yes, please." He returned his attention to the last two paragraphs on the Smartboard.

Charlimedes traveled to the island of King Minos, Keeper of the Golden Touch. Minos happily transformed a huge boulder into gold and then asked Charlimedes to do him a favor. "I would like for you to kick the giant egg of a harpy into the chariot of Apollo. This Harpy has been terrorizing my kingdom, and if Apollo has the egg in his chariot, he will take the egg to the other side of the world before the Harpy can get it back.

The next day, Charlimedes found the egg and ran at it at a speed that rivaled that of Atalanta herself. He swung his mighty leg with all his might... and he SUCCEEDED! The egg went flying up to the chariot of Apollo, which just happened to be going by at that time. Its mother followed in hot pursuit, and she disappeared into the depths of the sun.

Victorious Charlimedes took the golden boulder and traded it to Lucy for the guardian of the underworld, Tiberius. Then he traded Tiberius to Hades for his helmet of invisibility. Next, he traded Hades' helmet of invisibility to Ares for Athe-

na's pet owl of wisdom. Athena forgave him for smashing her marble statue, and Charlimedes was not cast into the depths of the underworld. The End."

Sheldon turned to the class, and I led a round of applause as I had always done when a student shared his or her writing. I told him he should be proud of the story. Now that it was finished, I invited the class to comment. The understanding here was that any criticism must be helpful, not hurtful, and with anything that was negative, there must also be something that was positive.

Several students raised their hands and made comments. Although each student followed the rules, Sheldon seemed a bit brow-beaten with each negative remark. He grew fidgety and agitated as he stood there, but I let the discussion continue.

Things seemed to be going along fine as I began to add my own praise to Sheldon's work, but with every positive dissection there inevitably would be some small criticism intended to help the student to make improvements. It began with a few minor considerations to make the story a little clearer. I would ask a question about an event in the story, and Sheldon would reply defensively. I pointed out one or two technical errors: He hadn't capitalized the first word of dialogue and had not used quotation marks to indicate the characters were speaking. Perhaps I missed it in Sheldon's eyes that he didn't like being told that there was anything wrong with his writing. When I mentioned the lack of quotes in front of the class, Sheldon gasped and said, "Well, I think it's pretty obvious that he was saying something."

His voice was loud, but not angry. As I pointed out a few more minor errors, he grew louder, explaining why he had done this. He began to interrupt me as I tried to discuss the piece. Only mildly annoyed with his behavior, and oblivious to his sensitivity, I plunged on.

"...And it looks like you've got a run-on sentence here," I pointed out. "That's something you can fix in revision."

"Actually," Sheldon corrected, "that's a comma splice."

And now I was irritated.

Although Sheldon was probably right, I scolded him for being disruptive, and at times, rude. I told him he was disrespectful for trying to correct me. I would have been harder on him, but he apologized almost immediately.

I have done many things the wrong way in my career as a teacher, and of all the things I have done, well, this is one of them.

Another teacher might have handled this situation differently. Gifted and Talented students are a different breed. They are unpredictable, and they often are overly sensitive to criticism. I finally understood that Sheldon was uncomfortable with being told that something he had done was not yet perfect. It suddenly occurred to me that he had really stuck his neck out allowing me to use his writing in the class.

This was a lesson for me, not him.

I eased off the tongue-lashing and reminded Sheldon that this was a distinguished piece of writing. Still stressed, and with the urgency of one who is about to wet his pants, he said, "Can I go to the computer lab and work on it? I want it to be exactly right."

I let him go.

The piece was distinguished when Sheldon completed it. Unfortunately, he only got a proficient score on his portfolio that year. You see, he was quite stubborn about revising any of his work, and he refused to make the changes that his editor had discussed with him. He felt that his work was already distinguished. He was extremely disappointed when he learned the overall score that he had received.

Nevertheless, I know that as an adult, Sheldon became a successful young man. I fully expect that one day, I will drive by an office building in a bigger city like Lexington, Kentucky, and out front I will see his name in big gold letters. Directly below the name, it will likely say, "Attorney at Law," or "Physician."

SMOKIN' IN THE BOY'S ROOM

The teachers at my school would jokingly refer to them as Butch and Sundance. Larry Bantam was the first of many principals I worked with in my twenty-two years at the Melungeon County Middle School. Steve Birch was his assistant principal, and about five years later he would become my second principal. They were the best tandem of supervisors I would ever have as a middle school teacher.

From the day I started working there, it was clear to me they were in control of the school. I still recall the vivid image of the two of them standing at the end of the hallway during classroom changes, Larry leaning against the wall like a gunslinger waiting for someone to slap leather, and Steve at his side with his foot propped up on the heater vent, looking equally dangerous. Larry was tall and slim in those days. His hair was blonde, and he usually approached everybody with a wide grin on his face and a friendly, "How ya doin'?" His country accent put me at ease whenever we spoke together. Steve was a bit more serious, but he had a good sense of humor. He was a bit under six feet tall, muscular, and had a bushy mustache like you might expect to see on a movie cowboy.

I liked working with these two supervisors who, unlike many other supervisors, made me feel like I was on the same team as they. They understood the value of a sense of humor on the job, which was and still is the best way to handle the daily stress of dealing with so many middle school students. From my first day as a teacher at this school, I felt comfortable walking into either of their offices, whether it was for help with a work-related problem, or just a social visit. I considered Larry and Steve two of my work friends.

Vardaman Faulkner was the eighth grader who was the thorn in each of their sides. I've no idea where his parents got the name, but it will forever stay in my mind as one given to a mischievous child. He was the only Vardaman I have ever met. For the sake of a name change in this story, I might have called him Ferris, or Huck, or maybe Spicoli, but his name was Vardaman, and I think he could have been the love child of all three and then something else.

Vardaman was a farmer's son. He often missed school to strip tobacco. He would occasionally skip school and use that as an excuse, but it didn't fly very well in the winter months. Vardaman didn't like school much, though he had a quick wit and was friendly and likable. You might say that he lived by his own rules. If he didn't agree with the rules that the school had made, he applied his own. He was often late to class, and while there he would talk to other students whenever he felt the need. If telling the truth to his teachers would get him into trouble, Vardaman would tell them something other than the truth. He had hit a growth spurt while still in elementary school, and by eighth grade he stood a slim and wiry six feet tall. He had shaggy brownish-red hair, and always kept a devilish grin on his somewhat acned face.

In his fourth period class, Vardaman often asked if he could go to the restroom. His teacher gratefully consented, knowing there would be less disruption to the class when he wasn't in it. While in the restroom, Vardaman would go into the first stall and light up a cigarette. He had spent quite a few days in after-school detention, but never for this offense. Standing so close to the toilet, he could simply drop the butt into the commode and flush it down as soon as he heard someone enter.

Larry and Steve knew Vardaman was smoking at school, and they were determined to catch him at it. They had tried and failed many times, but in the last month, Larry got the secret advantage he had been waiting on: The superintendent had provided him with a set of *walkie-talkies*. Keep in mind that this was 1995. People didn't carry phones around like they do today, so you couldn't send a text message or make a phone call while you were out of your office. A walkie-talkie was a two-way radio which would allow communication between two or more people in different (but nearby) locations. This was going to be the difference maker in catching Vardaman red-handed.

Larry handed Steve one of the two-way radios and kept the other.

"Just wait in the hallway for Vardaman to start

toward the restroom," he instructed, "When you see him, let me know."

Steve nodded, smiled, winked, and replied, "Happy hunting. I hope we get him this time."

Larry strode confidently toward the boy's restroom, turning up his radio and holding it to his mouth. "Check one, two... can you hear me okay?"

"Roger that. I can hear you fine," he grinned as he watched Larry fling open the bathroom door and go in it.

Fourth period class had started about ten minutes earlier, and Vardaman asked to be excused to go to the restroom. His teacher had just explained instructions for the day's lesson, but she handed him the hall pass and released him from the room. Vardaman walked into the hallway, took a few steps toward the restroom, and paused at the water fountain for a drink.

Steve stood at the far end of the hallway. He watched Vardaman bend toward the fountain and take a long drink. He glanced down the other hallway, where there was nothing more going on than a frustrated sixth grader fussing with her locker combination. Still looking at the sixth grader, he raised the radio to his mouth and whispered, "He's on his way."

Larry had his radio turned down low so he wouldn't be detected by the noise coming through it. He said, "Roger that."

Larry inserted the earpiece to avoid any potential squelch while he hid and listened for further updates on Vardaman's proximity. He went into a bathroom stall that was furthest from the entrance, pulling the door shut and latching it behind him. He noticed that if he stood at the door, he could easily see Vardaman come in because the door was only about five and a half feet tall. Larry wanted to wait where he couldn't be seen. There was also a gap beneath the bottom of the door and the floor, so he stepped up on the toilet seat. Vardaman would not see his feet.

The sound of the bathroom door opening caused Larry to crouch as he balanced on the seat. Vardaman's shoes squeaked gently against the tile floor. He stopped briefly at the mirror. Larry heard the squeaking of the faucet and water splashing. Then it stopped and Vardaman pulled at the towel dispenser several times more than he should have needed. He balled up the paper towel and pitched it toward the uncovered plastic garbage can. "Basket by Faulkner!" he whispered. His shoes resumed squeaking on the bathroom floor, and he seemed to move from one side of the bathroom to the other. Suddenly, it was very quiet. Larry glanced up from his crouched position on the toilet seat to the top of the door, where a set of brown eyes stared back at him.

"Hey, Mr. Bantam," Vardaman said. "How ya' doin'?"

Larry frowned and stepped down from the toilet seat. "Hiya, Vardaman," he mumbled. "You doin' okay?"

"I'm fine," he replied, with not the slightest hint of any concerns.

He didn't make any remark about the awkward situation as Larry slowly stepped down from the toilet seat, opened the door of the bathroom stall and stepped out.

Vardaman stepped back and walked to a nearby urinal. Knowing he had lost, Larry walked out of the bathroom without another word. He ambled down the hall toward where Steve stood expectantly.

"Did you get him?" Steve asked.

Larry smiled, then laughed. "You know," he said, "sometimes you get the bear, and sometimes the bear gets you."

He told Steve the story as the two of them watched Vardaman walk out of the bathroom and back up the hallway, glancing back and waving without a care in the world.

The two men laughed, as we all must laugh, and parted ways, to tend to their many other responsibilities.

I don't think Vardaman ever got caught smokin' in the boy's room. Hell, does it really even matter?

THE CRYSTAL BALL

Jewell came to the seventh grade with a reputation as a *behavior problem* student. It was generally little things, like talking during class, getting out of his seat without permission, or showing up to class without materials. Occasionally, he would reply sarcastically to a teacher, which often led to office referrals. Between him and his two older brothers, their mom was always in the office defending the behaviors of her boys and then tearfully confessing that they were guilty as charged. She couldn't get them under control at home either, she would say, but she promised that she would see to it that they were punished for their crimes, which, by the way, were generally misdemeanors and not felonious. Jewell already had been sent to the principal a few times this year for things like scribbling vulgar words into the text of a workbook or for shooting spit balls out of the end of a hollowed-out Bic pen.

He could also be very sweet. He was a cute, sandy-haired kid; smallish for his twelve years, but his head was a little large for his skinny frame, which seemed a good indicator of an eventual growth spurt. His remarkably blue eyes were constantly surveying the classroom and when the teacher's gaze locked onto his he would quickly look down at the assignment in earnest thought, and then resume his survey when she averted her eyes. He always had an impish grin on his face, which made him look that much more suspicious in a classroom.

Education just wasn't a priority for Jewell. This

was indicated by his C and D grades: good enough to pass, but he would never make the Dean's List. Social interaction and entertaining his friends were the things that mattered most to him.

One day, the cafeteria monitor sent Jewell to the principal's office for an incident that occurred during lunch. He was the only person sitting at the side of a table where, on the wall beside him, Hunt's mustard and ketchup packets had been squirted everywhere and then dumped on the floor under his seat. The evidence, though circumstantial, was against him.

Jewell had been waiting outside the principal's office for a while, as the principal was dealing with a more serious issue. The school psychologist, Dr. Rober, who knew Jewell and his family well, took the boy into his office to discuss what had happened. Jewell began by pleading the fifth.

Dr. Rober was a highly intelligent man. He also had a wonderful sense of humor. He and I had attended the University of Kentucky together, and he had been instrumental in my getting the job that started my public-school teaching career. His office contained the expected number of psychology books and college awards and degrees. He also had a couple of unusual posters on his office walls. He was an avid pipe smoker, and one poster showed a burning pipe and the words, *"Please be so kind as to hold your breath while I smoke."* The other poster was a print that represented different perspectives on what one is actually seeing: two vases if you look at it from one perspective, and two people about to kiss if you saw it from another. On his desk was a crystal ball which, when activated, you could ask a question and it would give a verbal response like "I'd say the chances are excellent." Or "It is highly unlikely."

As Jewell sat in the chair across from Dr. Rober, the two stared silently at each other. Jewell studied the psychologist's black hair, his salt-and-pepper beard and how his steady gaze seemed to look right into his soul. Finally, Jewell cried out, "That lunch lady is lyin'! She said I put mustard on the wall, but I didn't do nuthin'! It was like that when I got there!"

"Why do you think she said you put the mustard on the wall, Jewell?" Dr. Rober asked calmly, smiling like a Cheshire Cat.

"She doesn't like me! She thinks I'm always doin' things when her back is turned! She says I'm always tryn'a entertain my friends. I didn't do that, though, I swear!"

Dr. Rober turned to his crystal ball and good-naturedly he said, "You know, Jewell, my crystal ball is never wrong."

Jewell's eyes grew large and scared as he watched Dr. Rober reach for the sphere and say, "Let's see what the crystal ball says."

He waved his hand over the orb and murmured, "Crystal Ball, did Jewell put mustard and ketchup on the wall of the cafeteria?"

Dr. Rober removed his hand from above the crystal ball, and immediately it declared, "Without a doubt."

Jewell raised both his hands to his face, then fell forward onto Dr. Rober's desk. He took in a deep breath, and with a heavy sigh of resignation he groaned, "Them things ain't always right!"

It wasn't long before Jewell confessed to putting "at least some of the condiments" on the wall. While he was at it, he confessed to several other little cafeteria infractions, just to impress Dr. Rober. He even implicated some of his co-conspirators, because not very many seventh-grade boys like to be convicted alone.

There would be consequences that were sufficient to fit the crime, such as detention and a few days of eating his lunch outside the principal's office.

But the story didn't end here.

The following morning, Jewell's mom was waiting in the office when I signed in. I could see how agitated she was, so I thought I'd wait around for the vice principal, Mr. Birch, to come in from his morning duty directing bus traffic in the parking lot. Momma Bear was loaded for, well, bear.

She ambushed him when he came through the door of the front office, and blew past the attendance clerk, following him into his own office.

"I want to talk to that man who was doing that *hoo-dooey-voodoo* with my son!" she demanded.

Jewell's mom was a large, serious looking woman. She was just under six feet tall, but she was as round as she was tall, and could probably have tossed Dr. Rober through the wall if she wanted.

Grim-faced, Mr. Birch, Dr. Rober, and Jewell's mom all went into Dr. Rober's office, and I observed from a distance, listening from outside the room in which they sat. I didn't hear much and was about to leave for my scheduled class when I heard the laughter coming from the office.

I imagine Dr. Rober probably showed her the battery-operated crystal ball, and I guess she was satisfied with whatever he said to her. They eventually emerged from the office smiling and friendly.

Years later, Dr. Rober would recount this story to me and our wives over dinner. It was here I would learn that Jewell had told his mom that Dr. Rober had cast spells and called upon the devil. By this time, Dr. Rober would have moved on to a private practice, working with adolescents of all ages, and I would be several years from my own retirement. We would wonder where Jewell was now. Some kids move along and are never heard from again, and this was so of Jewell.

It was a priceless memory, and one that, when retold, makes me smile to this day.

A NICE MEMORY AT THE KENTUCKY KINGDOM

I was near the exit at the Kentucky Kingdom theme park when the cell phone in my pocket began to vibrate violently and sing out in its unique ring tone I had recently downloaded, a low-pitched male voice, singing, *"Please pick up the phone, oh won't you please pick up the phone?"*

"Hello?" I answered loudly because there was so much commotion and noise at Kentucky Kingdom that I had to shout just to hear myself. The place was packed with students from middle schools all over Kentucky and of all middle school ages. They laughed and talked loudly as they went from one section of the theme park to the next. This day was their reward for successful completion of the school year, and the dreaded state-wide testing assessments.

"Mr. Sexton?"- it was a voice I didn't recognize. The number was from my area code. "This is Mrs. Armstid. I'm a chaperone for your school today, and I'm at lunch with some of the kids."

"Hi Mrs. Armstid. I appreciate you for volunteering

your time to be here with us. Is everything okay?"

In the days when field trips could be "for fun," the teachers at my middle school would schedule a "reward day" at Six Flags, Kentucky Kingdom. This event was for students who had given their best effort on end-of-the-year state mandated testing and on *portfolios*, which were six (and later five) samples of their best writing assembled into one folder. We did this field trip for several years, but eventually administrators began to question the value of a reward for students who, in their words, "had done what they were expected to do."

The memory of these annual trips to the Louisville, Kentucky theme park stays with me to this day. They were great motivators for students. One trip stands out more than any other.

"Well," she said, "Yes, but I just wanted to find out if you have any money on reserve for kids who don't bring any. I'm with Vernon and Eula Tull, and both failed to bring any money for lunch."

I knew these two kids quite well. Vernon was a year older, but had failed back in sixth grade, putting him in the same grade as his little sister. He had been evaluated for special education at the end of that year and the assessment determined that he was dyslexic. How he managed to get through the previous grades is unknown to me, but kids with this kind of disability are surprisingly good at learning how to compensate. He was a sweet, shy boy with brown hair and bright blue eyes. He was about fifty pounds over his ideal weight, and he didn't seem to have many friends. He was almost six feet tall and made quite an imposing figure, but everybody knew that he was a marshmallow. Eula, on the other hand, was very social and friendly to everyone. She was oblivious to the sneers she sometimes got from the more popular kids. She stood all of 4'10" but her body was more developed than most girls her age, and she looked like a tiny adult woman. She didn't wear any make-up and her clothing looked like it had been handed down or purchased at the Goodwill. The one characteristic that did seem to match her brother was that her eyes were as blue as his.

Vernon and Eula were being raised by their single mom, and one could see they didn't have much just by looking at them. Their father had died from hepatitis a few years ago, and the home appliance business he owned closed almost immediately.

I was not surprised to hear that they hadn't brought any cash.

"Mrs. Armstid," I said, "would you send them to me, please? I'm standing by the exit from the park making sure nobody slips out without permission. I can't leave my area, but I'll see what I can do."

I only had about eighteen dollars in my pocket--- my own money. There was no budget for students who didn't have any money, and I knew that the school would not reimburse me for a cash purchase. Schools are not very trusting of teachers who make purchases and then ask to be compensated. As every teacher knows, if we didn't take the right steps, regardless of what we bought for our classrooms, we were quite unlikely to ever see that money again.

"Hey, Mr. Sexton!" Eula led her older brother to where I was standing. "Are you having a good time?"

She smiled widely and put out her closed fist. I punched it, then we made the firecracker gesture, wiggling our fingers rapidly.

"Hi Eula! Yeah, I'm living the dream!" I smiled. "How's it going, Vernon?"

Vernon grunted and smiled back.

"Did you guys forget to bring lunch money?" Eula continued to speak for them both.

"Mom said we would lose it if she gave it to either one of us. We're okay, though. We had a big breakfast."

I had my doubts that this was true.

"Well," I said, reaching for my wallet, "with all this exercise today, you need to keep up your strength."

I gave each of them nine dollars and said, "This should get you a drink and something to eat."

"Thank you!" they both said in chorus.

Eula threw a hug around my neck very suddenly and then the two of them trotted off to the concession area. A few minutes later, Eula ran back and, with a grin, pressed some leftover change into my hand.

The rest of the day passed along rather uneventfully. At about 1:30 everyone was supposed to meet in front of the gift shop near the exit where I had been stationed. This would get us back to school in time to load the busses and get students to their parents' waiting cars.

We had brought over 100 students and twenty parent chaperones along with six teachers. Each chaperone was responsible for five kids, and each teacher was responsible for four chaperones. I was responsible for assigning the teachers to stations throughout the park.

It was, in Robert Blake's own words, "The best

laid schemes o' mice and men."

As everybody gathered, I wandered over to a vacant spot on one of the benches by the gift store. Eula and Vernon were sitting on the bench. Beside them sat Mrs. Cora Tull, their mom!

"Hello Mrs. Tull!" I knew her first name, but we had only spoken once by phone and were not on a first name basis. I tried to conceal my surprise at seeing her here. "Are you a chaperone?"

The little woman, who looked like a much older and heavier version of Eula, smiled and said, "Yes, sweetie, I am," she smiled. "Eula and Vernon didn't think it was cool to let their mom be their chaperone, so I went with some other kids." She shifted a large package (obviously from the gift store) to the ground, making space on the bench so I could sit more comfortably. The contents of the package, an obscenely huge, stuffed animal, spilled out of the top of the three-foot-tall bag.

"What 'cha got there?" I asked.

"It's a stuffed animal, she grinned, excitedly, "I couldn't resist getting my little niece a souvenir since she didn't get to go on the trip with us. It will be a nice memory for us all."

I glanced at Eula, who was not paying any attention to our conversation. She was talking enthusiastically and with animated gestures to one of her recently acquired new friends. Vernon was sitting on the bench, his eyes darting from Eula to her friend, to me, and to his mom. He said nothing.

"That's great," I said, "I'm sure your niece will appreciate that you got it for her."

I had considered mentioning my eighteen dollars to Mrs. Tull, but knowing her struggle, I chalked it up to the many times I and other teachers had spent our own money on students knowing we would never get it back. Perhaps it's an investment; if not in this lifetime maybe in the next one.

We loaded the busses, knowing that everybody would be going home with many new memories and stories to tell about the end-of-the-year trip to the Kentucky Kingdom. The price of a good time had gone up for me just a little bit, but it was well worth it.

DELIVERANCE FROM THE CLASSROOM ROUTINE

July 8, 2012

Hi Mrs. Bundren,

I am writing you this email from a hotel in Curacao, where my wife and I are vacationing. Just wanted to congratulate you on being selected for the assistant principal's job at Melungeon County Middle School. I'm looking forward to working there with you! I know you will do a great job!

I heard through my co-workers in the seventh grade that there was a possibility that you might not approve the canoe trip for this year and wanted to weigh in and encourage you to allow it. I believe that the canoe trip is one of the best activities that a middle school student can do, not just because of how much fun it is, but also because it is a very educational activity that meets core content across the curriculum. It is also a motivational tool early in the school year because students must meet behavioral expectations to be allowed to go. The canoe trip is an educational activity disguised as a fun activity which every student who goes will remember long after he or she has graduated from high school. Ask any high school student about it and you'll get a glowing report.

While I'm sure I will forget to mention some of the educational advantages of the canoe trip, I'm going to go ahead and try to list as many as I can think of:

Language Arts: Every year the language arts teachers come up with a writing prompt for students after they have been canoeing. Sometimes the students write about their personal experience (narratives), sometimes they write an article about the environment (science), and sometimes they write a letter to someone (the principal, for example) about why an excursion like this one is so valuable and educational for a young person. There is always some kind of educational activity that connects the canoe trip to language arts. This also includes reading and vocabulary, too. I often encourage my students to read a book called Downriver, by Will Hobbs, which is about a group of young people who steal canoes from their wilderness leader and take them down the Colorado River. No, I'm not suggesting that students should ever steal canoes or get into the trouble these kids got into, but the book is a fun introduction to the excitement of paddling down a creek!

Science: This experience allows students to learn about their environment and the need for clean water, which supplies communities throughout the state with water to drink and water for their farmland. Some years we have invited park rangers or the original owner of Canoe Kentucky, Ed Council, to speak with students about the environment. Nathan Depenbrock, one of the owners, always talks about water safety and the importance of the waterways before launching students into the Elkhorn Creek. Students learn about life forms in the waterways of Kentucky, some good, and some bad. They learn what is polluting the waters and gain a healthy respect for our need to keep our waters clean. Also, they learn more about the water cycle, which is a huge part of our science curriculum in the seventh-grade year. Every year during testing I see students working on some kind of question over the water cycle and I'm thankful that they learned about it in part because of the canoe trip and the conversations the science teacher had with them following it.

Social Studies: Students learn how valuable waterways have been throughout history. They discover why ancient civilizations settled in an area close to water for their survival, and even invented early "plumbing" from these waters. They also learn about how explorers and native American Indians once paddled this same creek whose waters they will be navigating.

Math and Physics: When students are standing in shoulder-high water with their flipped canoe, they often try to raise their water-filled canoe out of the creek without understanding that because of the amount of water in it they will never succeed unless they raise it one side at a time. This gets into some complex thinking processes that require them to figure out they must raise one side at a time. Physics, proportions, weight, ratios, reasoning skills, etc., are addressed on this trip.

Physical Education: The value of physical education cannot be overstated for the canoe trip. Some students will never get to do something like this again for the rest of their lives, so it is a valuable experience. Some will enjoy it so much that they will do it again and perhaps become skilled with watercraft like the canoe. The physical activity will be good for them for obvious reasons. Over the years we've seen obesity become a more serious problem in our country and Kentucky seems to be leading the way. Canoeing is excellent exercise!

Cooperative Learning: Almost all of the teachers who have been at Melungeon County for more than a few years have had training in Spencer Kagan's Cooperative Learning Model. Nothing requires cooperative learning skills more than an experience like canoeing with a partner. Social skills are encouraged through the "out of the comfort zone" activity of selecting someone with whom to be partnered. Students are encouraged to be supportive to each other as they struggle with learning the new activity. Some step up and assume the responsibility for others who are not as skilled. Students learn how to steer and power the canoe, working as one to go up and down the creek. They learn how to get on and off the canoe without flipping it. To be honest, this is the most difficult part of the experience for teachers. We want students to work together without being told to do so because this is more of a "real-life activity." I have seen some students do this perfectly, and others who grew so infuriated with their partner that I had to put them in another canoe. Fortunately, we have always had plenty of teacher and parent cooperation in the supervision of these young people and with a little intervention we have kept the problems in check.

I hope that this email has convinced you that the canoe trip is a worthwhile learning activity for our Melungeon County students. It has been a tradition for so many years that some of us have just assumed we would do it without needing to go through the approval process. At the end of the last school year, I scheduled it for September 4, 5, and 9, and 10th this school year. The plan is to allow students to sign up for the day that is most convenient for them so they can go with their close friends. Those who stay back will have academic activities in a different, combined rotation of classes. Sign-ups for the trip have to happen pretty quickly and we need parent volunteers and other school staff (you and the other administrators in the building have filled this role in the past) to commit to going along for better *supervision.*

I'm sorry this has been such a long email. I collect my thoughts in an email better than I do speaking and I guess I have a lot of thoughts on this topic.

Thanks!

Randy Sexton

*There was no response to this email. The canoe trip request was denied, and future canoe trips were not permitted, until...

August 8, 2015

"This one is on you, Mr. Sexton,"

Mrs. Bundren, who would be the final school counselor and assistant principal under whom I would work in my twenty-two-year career at Melungeon County Middle School, scowled at me from her captain's chair. I sat across from her desk in a hard, wooden seat, pretending to be oblivious to her smoldering rage, but well-aware of what I had done to cause it.

Mrs. Bundren was a tall, slender woman of thirty-eight years. Her hair was cut in a Pixie cut, close to her ears and well above the collar of her blouse, and because of the lack of any contours to her breasts or hips, it would have been easy to mistake her for a boy. Her skin was a rather pale white, as if she had seldom gone out in the sunlight. She may not have been a vampire, but there were many times when it seemed she really did suck the life out of me. She had never been married, but when her mood was good, she would talk about the many cats she had in her home. She had been a classroom teacher in Wolf County, Kentucky, for eight years and an assistant principal for one before being hired in Melungeon County for her first job as both assistant principal and school counselor. It was her responsibility to conference with students and to approve teacher requests for reimbursements and field trips. Word had gotten out that she was something of a control freak before I ever laid eyes on her. One of the teachers had a friend in Wolf County who had told her this. I soon discovered that it was true.

In my first year of teaching in Melungeon County, the other teachers had decided that in the first month of school, students needed a super-cool "field trip." This had to be something that would get them away from the daily routine of sitting in a classroom. It had to be an excursion away from the school that they could earn with their good behavior in those early days of classes. It had to be something that would motivate them to want to go on future field trips. And it had to be something that they would come home from at the end of the day saying, "*Man, I had fun!*"

Many ideas had been kicked around before we decided that the best option was to take large groups of students to the Elkhorn Creek in Georgetown, Kentucky, and put them in canoes.

This would be an "educational" experience: students would learn about wildlife, the conditions and purity of the water, the tributaries that emptied into the Kentucky River and elsewhere, and many other things connected to science, history, literature (students would write about their experiences), and much more. It would be a good social experience because there would be at least two students in each canoe, learning how to work together to navigate their canoe up and down the narrow, slow-moving creek.

One of the teachers, Mr. Christian, had a connection to a family-owned canoe rental company called *Canoe Kentucky*. Ed Counsel and his daughter Allison were the owners of the business. Because I was in my first year in this school district, I didn't have very much responsibility. All I had to do was show up for school on the morning of the trip and help supervise the students along with three to four other teachers, ten to twelve parent volunteers, and eighty to one hundred twelve-year-old seventh graders who didn't even have to know how to swim, because they would wear life jackets the entire time.

Little did I know that in the years to come, this excursion would become my responsibility. Mr. Council would retire, and his daughter would marry an outdoor naturist named Nathan Depenbrock. For the next twenty years I would call them before the start of the new school year to reserve four school days surrounding the Labor Day weekend, and we would plan out the canoe trip. I began to think of Nathan and Allison as friends, although I would only ever see them at this time of the year.

There are many stories I could share about the yearly canoe trip. I have asked the teachers that I worked with to share a few memories of their canoe trips, and one day I hope I can share some of their tales of adventure along the Elkhorn Creek, in Georgetown, Kentucky.

One of my own recollections was the very last canoe trip. Ever since the first time we took our seventh graders canoeing, the administration, starting with the superintendent of schools, our school principal, the assistant principal, and the school counselors, all agreed that this was one of the best activities we had ever come up with for our students. I recall that I had been through at least seven different principals by my twenty-second year and four different school superintendents. There had been God only knows how many different assistant principals, and in recent years there had been multiple changes in teachers, who had moved to different grades, gone to work in other districts, or decided to move on to another career.

Most of them had supported the idea of doing the canoe trip, but as time passed, the thinking about the educational value of time outside of the classroom had begun to change. Our academic scores had faltered slightly in state-wide testing compared to many other districts (we were never below the "average," but this was not acceptable).

Mrs. Bundren was hired to be the assistant principal four or five years before I retired. Her promise was to raise our state-wide assessment scores, and to her credit, she accomplished that. Some staff found her style to be a bit abrasive, though. She was not "warm and fuzzy" like the assistant principal before her. She was not particularly friendly to any of the teachers, as far as I know, although over time she became friends with some that were more aligned with her way of running things. She was strict with teachers and gave far more negative feedback than positive feedback in her first few years. She often took the side of an angry parent before conferencing with a teacher about an incident with a misbehaving student.

Regardless of the life jackets all students had to wear, she did not want the teachers to take students on a field trip that involved putting two or three of them in a canoe into a creek that was six or seven feet deep in places. There were spiders, ticks, and snakes in the tree branches hanging over the water. This activity would take students out of the classroom environment for an entire day that could be used for academic instruction.

This attitude rubbed me the wrong way.

I grudgingly accepted the end to our canoe trip for a couple of years. I had met with Mrs. Bundren several times trying to convince her that this was a valuable experience for the students, but I felt like I was talking to a wall the entire time. She had made up her mind. New seventh graders who had heard about how much fun their older brother or sister had on the curvy, jewel-blue Elkhorn Creek were very disappointed to learn that they would not be going.

Unfortunately, going on field trips in general had grown less acceptable over the years, and there were other disappointments to come that distracted them from their displeasure over this one.

In general, school had become less a thing to look forward to over the years. Many of the fun, interactive classroom activities were decreasing in favor of direct instruction. Not that teachers couldn't try to make it fun, but some of the techniques we had been using to get students out of their seats, moving around the classroom, and teaching one another were becoming obsolete.

In Mrs. Bundren's third year as assistant principal, I had been moved from seventh grade Language Arts to sixth grade Language Arts. It was not a big difference in what I was teaching or how I was teaching it. I was teamed with several teachers I liked very much. Mr. Caine, who taught math and somehow still managed to be a favorite of the students, was the first of them to bring up the idea that we should consider bringing back the canoe trip. I was surprised to hear a few of the other teachers agree with him. I thought the canoe trip was long forgotten, but here were several younger teachers expressing some enthusiasm for bringing it back!

Before the start of the school year, I submitted the documentation that was required to request permission for this field trip. I had justified this excursion as an educational experience, laying on the same language I used at the start of this narrative.

One could say I went around Mrs. Bundren with the paperwork, because instead of putting it in her box, I dropped it off at the board of education's office, where it would be seen by the superintendent of schools before Mrs. Bundren saw it.

Did it make any difference that the superintendent had a daughter in the sixth grade that year?

I don't know, it might have.

The field trip was approved a few days before the start of classes. It didn't escape my attention that Mrs. Bundren wouldn't speak to me in the hallways and only spoke to me that day in her office long enough to say that if anything bad happened, I would be the one responsible.

But the canoe trip was ON!

Our trip happened on Thursday and Friday before

Labor Day, and then Tuesday and Wednesday after Labor Day. Each day we would take eighty or so students, a few teachers, some parents (whose criminal background checks had checked out), and one or two other volunteers to Great Crossings Park in Georgetown, Kentucky, and meet our friends from Canoe Kentucky at the launch area just fifty yards above a little man-made waterfall.

This part of the creek had a pretty checkered past as only a mile south of where we were putting in there had once been a body dumped about a mile downstream from the direction we were paddling. It was a murder case, and the body had been discovered during one of our scheduled times on the water. This, of course, led to one or two panicked parents calling the school to find out which of their children had been murdered.

There had also been several drownings at the waterfall in years gone by, and one of them was a boy who had once been one of our students. The boy had even gone with us for a canoe trip several years earlier. He had gone to the creek with friends and tried to walk across the five-foot waterfall. He fell in, and he didn't ever come back up. As time went by there were rumors that his drowning had happened during one of our canoe field trips, but those rumors were patently false.

To this day, there is a monument dedicated to that young man right beside the waterfall where he drowned. I will never forget his smiling, friendly face.

Each day of this trip was a huge success. The weather was perfect, the water was not too high or low, and although there were students who appeared to be afraid of what dangers may have been lurking in the depths of the creek, I don't remember anybody complaining that they didn't enjoy the outdoor experience we had taken them on. Students returned to the school muddy and smelling of the creek, but each of them seemed to have a fun story to share with those who had not gone on this day or with others who would be going after them.

There were definitely a few minor incidents on each day of the canoe trip: I remember well the two boys who couldn't figure out how to paddle up the stream and spent most of their time crashing their canoe into the side of the muddy bank, flipping out, and, once they were back in their canoe, paddling to the other side. Wash, rinse, repeat…

Eventually they figured it out.

I will never forget Cynthia, who easily weighed 300 pounds, and was much too large for a canoe. She spent most of her time in it screaming for help. She continued to do this from one end of the creek to the other. Bless her heart, she was never in any danger, but she had never been in a creek or a canoe and everything about this day was new and terrifying to her.

One of the most potentially dangerous moments occurred when I paddled up to two boys who were arguing over how to navigate their canoe. Both boys were very immature and were somehow thrown together because nobody else wanted to canoe with them. Clinton was standing in the canoe, holding his paddle over his head in preparation to bash Burt's skull in. Burt held his own paddle in each fist like an oak staff, preparing to block the blow. Fortunately, the cool-headed parent who intervened calmed them down, and I put Clinton in my canoe while Burt had to navigate his canoe alone.

Of everything I have ever done as a teacher in Melungeon County, Kentucky, the canoe trip at the Elkhorn Creek is my legacy.

Many years after the first canoe trip, I have had the good fortune to run into old students, some of them now adults with their own children. They rarely remember that I taught them about Edgar Allan Poe, or Shel Silverstein. They occasionally recall that they had learned about Greek mythology in my classroom. They almost always tell me what a great time they had with that outdoor experience the day we went canoeing on the Elkhorn Creek.

DIFFERENT STREAMS OF CONSCIOUSNESS

CO-WRITTEN BY RANDY SEXTON AND MERIDETH PITTMAN

I had been at Melungeon County Middle School for quite a few years when Mrs. Pittman joined the staff. She was a first-year teacher, young, pretty, and energetic. She was only about five feet tall, and was occasionally mistaken for one of the students, many of whom were taller than she. She was easy-going and her kids said she was fun. Honestly, she was just what the rest of the teachers needed to inject our veins with some enthusiasm. And she was thrilled to learn that in the seventh grade, we took the kids canoeing.

Mrs. Pittman would spend several years teaching in Melungeon County before jumping ship (or should I say, *canoes?*) to teach in neighboring Boyle County. She would struggle through some physical troubles and surgery during this time too. She would survive the normal problems of everyday life, marriage, and parenthood. And she would never forget the years she took students canoeing down the Elkhorn Creek with me and many other teachers.

In preparing to write this book, I asked some of the teachers I had worked with to share their most memorable moments of the times we took the students canoeing. When I asked Mrs. Pittman if she would tell me about some of her memories of canoeing with the kids, she was excited. It's good when you, the reader, can get the story from a different stream of consciousness than I, your humble narrator, can provide.

Here, then, in her own words, are some of the memories Mrs. Pittman shared with me regarding those wonderful times:

"In my first year as a middle school teacher, I learned that my seventh graders would be going on an annual field trip at some time near the start of the year. I was thrilled! I wasn't particularly experienced, and I was nervous about keeping up with the kids. I also knew that if something bad happened under my supervision I would lose my job for sure.

When the day of the trip came, I partnered up in my canoe with my classroom neighbor, Mrs. Johansson, who taught Language Arts and had a few more years under her belt as a teacher. It was a beautiful September day, and we watched as most of the students struggled to figure out how to operate their canoes. We laughed as kids paddled in circles, got hung up on the bank, and sometimes they capsized their canoes. Their life jackets kept them afloat and the teachers and volunteers came to their rescue and got them on their way again. Most of these kids had never been in a canoe, and probably never would again, but they absolutely loved it!

After a couple of miles, Mrs. Johansson and I rowed to the bank and let the kids get out and play in the shallow water. It occurred to me that they might make their way to the deeper waters of the creek, so I swam out to the middle, where the water reached my waist. All of us were wearing life jackets. I made sure nobody went past where I stood.

As I watched the kids splash around and play, I thought about how I knew I had made the right career choice. I had only been a teacher for a month, but I couldn't imagine myself doing anything else. I felt a responsibility to these kids, not only to be their history teacher, but to be their protector. I would make sure they were safe, taken care of, and would know that I would always be there for them."

One year, the rain had been particularly bad before our planned canoeing excursion. My own memory of this canoe-trip-turned-rafting adventure is a bit different from Mrs. Pittman's, but only because for much of the time we were far apart as we hurtled down the flooded creek.

This was probably the most exciting of all our trips to Elkhorn Creek.

"I remember one year it had rained a lot, and we kept having to reschedule our annual canoe trip. Finally, the Canoe Kentucky people decided since the water levels were so high, we could take rafts. I am athletic and pretty adventurous, but I was scared to death at the thought of being the "captain" of a raft full of middle school kids. I immediately recruited a group of softball girls because I figured they would get the hang of things quickly. I remember Mrs. Johansson freaking out in her witty, dramatic way, which only added to my nervousness.

We launched ourselves boldly into the swollen creek. The other teachers and their kids had gone ahead of us, and there was one parent in a kayak whose job it was to "take up the rear" and make sure everybody got safely to the end of the creek. Somehow, he got confused about his role, because he left us far behind as soon as we got in the creek. I had six of the strongest girls rowing through the splashing water. Things were going well at first, but then the current picked up and we really had to row and maneuver through some debris in the water. I heard Mrs. Johansson, a dozen yards behind us, squealing and panicking, saying, "Oh, I wasn't cut out for the canoeing life! I want this to be over!" Mrs. Johansson had recruited some of the football players on her raft. It was a smart move, but they seemed as clueless as my girls were. I heard her ask Bryce, one of the biggest boys, to switch places with her so he could be the "leader." A look of relief flooded her face as Bryce guided the raft down the creek and past my girls.

My own raft drifted dangerously close to the bank and we couldn't get away from the downed trees and limbs that dangled dauntingly over our heads and across the water. I screamed at my girls, "DUCK!", but Alyssa, my second baseman, was hit by a branch and was flung into the water!

I leaped from my spot in the back of the raft and leaned over, grabbing her by the back of her life jacket. She was screaming, and so was I. In fact, everybody on the raft was screaming! I don't think she was ever in any real danger because the water was only a couple of feet deep here, but her legs were being pulled under the raft, and she was hysterical. I yelled for the girls to help me get her out of the water. The catcher, shortstop, and two outfielders helped me grab Alyssa and pull her back into the raft.

My heart was pounding, and all the girls kept scream-

ing, but we got Alyssa back in the raft.

Alyssa, exhausted and no longer able to scream, curled up in the middle of the raft.

"I could have drowned," she whimpered, dramatically "You all saved me!"

She repeated this several more times. I assured her she was fine and that she wouldn't have drowned.

In all the chaos, Alyssa's oar floated downriver, forever lost to the creek. She sat in the center of the raft as we sailed on to the final stop at the Canoe Kentucky office. By the time we were safely on land, Alyssa would be contentedly eating an ice cream cone from the little shop inside the building.

Mrs. Johansson was waiting for us with her big, strong football players. She smiled widely and asked, "Did you all have fun?"

The girls all cried out, "NO!"

But in a day or two they would be talking about how they all had the time of their lives, and how they had saved Alyssa's life.

Once we paddled back to shore and got off the boat, I couldn't decide if that was fun, or terrifying. I was glad it was over, though. Besides Mrs. Johansson and me, none of the other teachers had any issues with the rafts. We laughed to hear of the calmness and serenity of the other teachers and students who, it seemed, had gone on a totally different field trip.

Although I know she felt safe with her crew of football players, Mrs. Johansson and I made a pact for all future field trips to the Elkhorn Creek: No more rafts!"

Merideth and I did have a vastly different experience each time we went canoeing with the students. Each of these was fun and memorable. I hope to share more about this in future tales of canoeing the Elkhorn Creek.

CANDACE

"Hey Mr. Sexton, want to see me do my back hand-spring?"

Candy smiled confidently and glanced around the flat, grassy park for a good place to show me the move she had been perfecting.

We had just come from the seventh-grade ca-noeing trip at Elkhorn Creek to Cove Spring Park with about eighty other students and staff who were exhaust-ed from the day's adventure. Candy and several of her friends were walking on the nature trails as a concluding part of our first and best field trip of the year. I was tag-ging along as their teacher/chaperone.

"Just as long as you promise you won't hurt your-self," I replied, "I couldn't live with myself if you got hurt showing me your skills."

"I won't get hurt," she said with complete confidence. "I do this all the time. Do you want me to do a running back handspring, or a standing one?"

I tried to decide which of these sounded least danger-ous and said, "Standing?"

Candy moved to a clear area and did her move. I

watched as she flipped head over heels and landed perfectly on both feet. I knew nothing about gymnastics or cheerleading, but I praised her for completing it without breaking her neck. She smiled proudly and said, "Next year, I'm going to be a cheerleader for the eighth grade!"

Back in August of this seventh-grade year, Candace had been the first student to speak to me. The new seventh graders were in the gymnasium for the opening day of school. Candace was on the list of names for my first period World Literature class, and as I called out the names, she had come to the front of the line.

"It's Candy." She said firmly.

"Excuse me?" I said, surprised by her assertiveness.

"Nobody calls me Candace," she said firmly, "It's Candy."

She positioned herself in front of me as we prepared the *"single file, no talking"* line to walk to the seventh-grade wing of the building.

"Are you a good leader?" I asked her.

She didn't know me well enough yet to pick up on the playful tone of my voice.

"I guess," she said cautiously.

There was a slight defensiveness in her tone, which I ignored. Most of the seventh graders were still very nervous to be changing from sixth grade to seventh and Candace was no exception.

"I want you to lead this group to my classroom, 703. Keep everybody single file and quiet. When you get there, you are in charge, okay?"

"Ohhh-kay." She replied.

REACHABLE MOMENTS   **79**

She still wasn't sure about me, but she smiled broadly, appreciating her new position of authority. She whispered something to a friend in the line behind her and the friend giggled.

During that first semester, twelve-year-old Candy and I got to know one another well. She began to trust me as more of a friend than a teacher. She was warm and friendly with her friends and with me, but she also had the occasional mean streak, especially with those she didn't like. She was pretty, too, with raven hair and the deepest blue eyes. That meant that the boys would be competing for her attention and creating the usual drama for the green-eyed monster that circulated the halls of the seventh grade. She seemed to have a preference for the boys who were risk-takers and rebels, and she occasionally got in trouble at school as a result.

That first semester came and went very quickly. I lost Candy to the class changes that always happen at mid-year. She went from my literature class, where we had studied Greek mythology, Shakespeare, Poetry and writing, to another teacher's grammar class, where they studied nouns, verbs, and adjectives.

Every now and then, Candy would sneak away from a class and hang out in my room. She didn't usually stay long, but she took time to write something on the board, like, *Candy Loves You, Mr. Sexton!!!* before returning to whatever class she was supposed to be attending.

Once, during my planning period, Candace came to the room with her friend, Ashley, and there were two other girls already there, visiting me the same as Candy liked to do. The girls didn't like each other much, and while Candace and Ashley were writing rude things about them on one board in the room, Katie and Amber were writing equally ugly things about them on the other. It was an awkward moment for me, but I divided my attention equally to the young girls and let them trade the insults without getting involved.

It came to nothing. In another week those same girls would be the best of friends.

Late in the school year, Candy came to my room and said, "Mr. Sexton, I'm moving. I'm going to another school in Owenton."

"Really?" I said, "Why? What school are you going to?"

"My mom and dad are getting divorced. I'm going to go stay with my dad now. I'll be going to Forks of Elkhorn Middle School. My mom is moving in with my Meema, so I might be back some day."

At this time, Forks of Elkhorn Middle had a reputation for frequent fights in the hallway and disruptions in the classroom. I was sad to hear she was leaving. "That's not as good a school as Melungeon Middle," I told her, although I was actually thinking out loud.

"I know."

Candy had lived a life that hardened her emotions, and rarely expressed it when she was sad, but the tear rolling down her cheek betrayed her.

The lump in my own throat was not as obvious, but it was there just the same.

I gave Candy my email address and told her to stay in touch, knowing that they rarely do. I was unhappy to say good-bye. I hoped there would be a teacher to keep

driving off. At some point, she and her friends left, and crossed a couple of very busy streets, finally crossing a freeway, to get through a fence that led to the subdivision where one of the boys lived. About the same time, a storm had moved in, and severe weather alerts were up all-around the county. I'm told that her grandma had called her cell phone and said she was going to pick Candy up because the weather was getting worse. There had been several lightning strikes nearby, and concerns of a tornado hitting the area were growing.

Unfortunately, Candy was no longer there, and she wasn't going to tell her grandma that she was at the home of a boy her grandma didn't know. I'm told that Candy and her friends were trying to get back to the Hairy Monkey so her grandma would meet them there and they wouldn't have to explain what they were doing at the boy's house.

The rain was coming down in a torrential downpour when they left the house. They wanted to get back to the entertainment center before Candy's grandma got there, so they hurried back the way they had come. As Candy tried to cross the Interstate Freeway, she was struck by a car driven by a twenty-five-year-old man.

She died immediately.

It wasn't the man's fault. Nobody can be blamed for hitting a pedestrian on a freeway, late at night, and in a severe thunderstorm. All the other kids survived, but I never heard a thing about them. I can only imagine their horror.

The death of any child crushes the soul of the community, and Candace's death crushed the souls of the two that she had lived in over the last few months. Her family was devastated. So were her friends. So was I. The television news showed her distraught aunt talking about what happened and her grandma posted an agonizing response to an internet news story that had spread insensitive gossip about the kids.

The true story came in bits and pieces. I first heard rumors from people in the community. One of Candy's friends texted me and gave a few more details. The local news reported that a girl had been killed on the freeway, but details were not available pending notification of the family. I received an "all-call" voicemail from my principal the next morning. The recorded message reported that Candace had been killed in a car accident, but I already knew that.

I spent the rest of the weekend getting different information from different people.

Another one of my students had begun texting me and she gave me her version of the story. She hadn't been with Candy, but had seen her with her friends at the entertainment center.

I spoke to other teachers and gleaned what little I could.

It seemed that I already knew more than most of them.

On Monday, there were kids crying all morning long. Most of them knew how close I was to Candy, and they came to me to grieve. I don't know how comforting my words to them were. I was hurting just as much.

Candy's parents came to school later that day and asked me if I could speak at her funeral because I was her favorite teacher. I did as they asked, but even at the funeral I was numb and didn't know what to say. I was still processing her death.

Standing in front of all the grieving people, I told them how devastating it was for all of us to lose a young member of our community, and a person with so much potential. I told a couple stories about how she used to come into my classroom at times when she wasn't supposed to be there. A few people laughed, knowing that the girl I was describing was so much their beloved Candy. I talked about how much everybody loved her.

And then I stopped.

I didn't know what else to say. I was in midthought, but I couldn't say anything more.

I walked back to my pew and sat next to some of the other teachers that had come with me. I felt like I hadn't said enough about how special Candy really was, but the funeral proceeded. It was comforting to be with so many people who loved Candace.

I used to roll my eyes when a student would write something corny about *living for today because tomorrow is not promised to us,* but this was the truth for Candy. There is nothing positive to take from this tragedy. Obviously, Candy shouldn't have been where she was, and she shouldn't have lied to her grandma about what she was really doing. What sticks in my head the most, however, is that Candy had such a future ahead of her. She was on her way to becoming all that she could have been. Now we'll never know what that was. I'll never forget Candy, or Seth, or Charles, or Jodi, or the many other students who lost their lives during the years I was a teacher at

Melungeon County. Every teacher faces these kinds of tragedies during their careers.

The hardest part of being a teacher is having to stay strong for the kids who were still with me and knowing that the path ahead really could end at any time.

LEARNING NOT TO SPEAK WAH

In the 2012/2013 school year, my teaching team had one of my favorite groups of students ever in the seventh grade. Many were children of teachers throughout the county, and these devoted students had influenced others in the ways of good classroom behavior and the importance of academic success. Parents were interested in their child's achievement and the atmosphere often was one of mutual respect and support.

As the year progressed, however, I began to see some of the same problems as I had often encountered with other students in the past. One problem was that the students were not looking at me when I was teaching. Some, though their faces were turned toward me, had tuned me out. I had become what I call the "Charlie Brown teacher."

Remember the speaking sound made by the teacher in the old Charlie Brown cartoons? "Wah-wah wahwahwah-WAH-wahwah-WAH-Wahwa-wha?"

This is what my students seemed to be hearing as I spoke to them now.

This became more evident at the end of the semester,

when I gave my students the final on the novel we had finished, *The Lightning Thief,* by Rick Riordan. When the bell rang to start class, I passed out the bubble sheets and guided everyone through the process of filling them out. Then I pointed to the board, where I had written the instructions for the writing prompt:

For the written response, you are to write about the plot of our novel. Begin by discussing the settings of the story. Describe 3-5 of the conflicts before writing about what the climax of the novel is. Finally, discuss the falling action of the novel and how the loose ends are resolved by the end of the story. If you need paper, there is some at my desk, where you are to leave your graded bubble sheet.

I felt comfortable with the assignment. We had discussed the elements of fiction and plot development many times in the last nine weeks, and twice this week. Several responses to the questions were possible, but students would have to show me what they knew about the book. The previous Tuesday students picked up the study guide as they entered the classroom. A rousing session of review ensued as they gathered in groups of four to discuss the book. I had circulated around the room and joined each group as needed. The same writing prompt that would be on the test was on it.

Today was Thursday, so I had provided time for them to study the guide outside of class too. Friday would be available for students who might need a little more time to finish.

To make the test-taking process less painful, I allowed students to get up from their seats and scan their own bubble sheet when they finished. This gave them an opportunity to stretch their legs, snicker at one another for putting the response sheet in sideways (a good laugh should help them relax), see how they were doing on the first part of the test, and go back to their desk with good blood flow to their brains.

This seemed to work for most of the students.

However, in each class, I noticed a disturbing trend that got worse as the day went on: after scanning their bubble sheets, some students were returning to their desks and doing nothing but looking around the room!

To avoid embarrassing the ones who had forgotten to do the writing assignment, I made a general announcement, which probably distracted a few of my test-takers who were concentrating on their final.

"Don't forget to do the written part of the test when you give your graded bubble sheet to me," I whispered loudly.

In one class, I noticed that a boy continued to sit at his desk without starting on the writing section. This was Benjy, one of my lower achieving students: a good kid but he did not like school. Or teachers. Or other kids. I approached him gently. "Benjy, why aren't you doing the writing prompt?"

"I don't have any paper," he mumbled with a trace of attitude. His eyes met mine and I thought there was a bit of a challenge in them.

I ignored the challenge and said, "There is paper on my desk."

Benjy glanced across the room at my desk, but he didn't move, so I got the paper for him.

I unintentionally let a sigh of exasperation escape my mouth as frustration churned inside me.

Benjy began writing his name, the date, and the class he was in. I returned to the front of the class.

In my final class of the *day*, there were at least five Benjie's who didn't know there was a written section to do after the multiple-choice section.

Finally, caving in to my frustrations, I said, "Are you guys hearing anything I say in class? I'm starting to feel like Charlie Brown's teacher!"

I should add that I wasn't really all that angry. In fact, I was grinning when I said this, so nobody was particularly alarmed. They looked back at me blankly. *Charlie Brown? Which class is he in?* I was making a reference that was outdated for them.

It occurred to me that this was the age of *Honey Boo Boo*, not *Charlie Brown.*

As it dawned on the five Benjy's that I was speaking to them, they slowly fumbled about for paper. They smiled sheepishly and glanced at one another, then began the writing. A couple of them later admitted that they hadn't remembered that I said there was a writing section or that I had told them about it at the start of class.

Sorry, guys. I was speaking Wah.

HOW TO AVOID SPEAKING WAH

I need to practice what I preach. I know there are many ways to make sure the kids hear what I am saying, and sometimes I use these techniques. Usually, I just expect them to listen because I am so remarkably interesting! (Yes, I'm kidding.)

I have a few suggestions for teachers who want to learn how to avoid speaking Wah:

1. Make eye contact with all students when you are teaching. Be sure they are looking back at you.
2. Say a student's name to him or her during the instructional time.
3. Interrupt your lesson with questions directed at random students. Sometimes the questions don't even need to be about the lesson. This is just to get their attention focused back on the teacher.
4. Move around the room. Look for class work from another subject, notes the students are trying to pass, artwork they are attempting to put on their desks, and books they are reading. Make them put all this away and pay attention.
5. If you see a student talking to another student during your lesson, stop teaching, tell the student that the teacher needs the attention of the student they are distracting, and ask them to wait until a more appropriate time to continue their conversation. This

is a first warning. The response of the student is your clue as to where it goes from here.

6. Check for understanding. Students will not always admit that they don't know what you said, even though every word they heard was "Wah." If you have doubts, ask them to repeat the instructions back to you.

"WHY YA GOT THAT BIRD, FOR?"

It was a week before Halloween, and I had been shopping at one of my favorite stores, Halloween Express. I came home with two small skulls that had a light up candle whose red wax would ooze out of the eyes as it melted. I found big black spiders attached to a string that could dangle from the ceiling. I found cut-out bats for the door of my classroom. And I found a big, battery-operated raven. It would make a rolling "Caw" every time it was tapped on its keel. I was ready to teach the class nearly everything I knew about Edgar Allan Poe.

Teaching scary stories in Melungeon County Middle School had always been fun for me. The school had been built on an old Shaker village from the 1800's, and all that remained on the property was an historic graveyard. The graveyard was surrounded by a five-foot-tall stone barrier and had an entrance where the school had put up a gate to protect the gravestones from vandalism. It was roughly thirty yards from the back door of the seventh grade wing, and on Fridays the teachers would frequently take the students outside to play in the open fields of the largely forested area. The graveyard gave a certain creepiness to the school, and when rumors began to circulate that the school was haunted with the ghosts of the buried, we sometimes played that up for the fun stories we would study such as Edgar Allan Poe's "The *Raven.*"

A couple days before the lessons began, my wife, Jackie, had sewn the raven to the shoulder of my shirt. It had been a lot of work to get the raven to stand up straight. But Jackie was an expert seamstress, and her skill paid off.

That Monday before the thirty-first, I perched myself in the hallway outside my classroom, greeting the seventh-grade students as they arrived for their morning classes. I appeared to be oblivious to their strange looks as they passed by me on their way to the first classes of the day. I would see each of them soon. Some students drew closer to get a better look. Others cringed away in fear, unsure if the thing was alive or not. Deontay, one of the bolder students, stopped in front of me with two Betas trailing him and said, "Sup', Mr. Sexton. Why you got that bird for?"

"Hi, Deontay." I said, smiling. "What bird is that?"

He laughed. "The one on your shoulder!"

I glanced around, first to the incorrect side and then to the other, pretending to see nothing. Deontay reached his hand to the bird, grazing it lightly, and then pulled back when the eyes lit up red and it made a gurgling, throaty sound. I pretended to hear nothing.

"Have a great day, boys. See you in class in a little while." I said, turning and going back into my classroom.

My first period students had already settled into their

seats and were looking at me anxiously. I posted my attendance and ignored their questions about the raven. Then I continued the lesson.

"Today," I said, "We are going to read a poem by Edgar Allan Poe called *"The Raven."* How many of you have heard of Poe?"

Madison raised her hand and before I had a chance to call on her, she said, "Mrs. Carris taught a story called *"The Tell-Tale Heart"* in fourth grade. It was cool!" A few other students who had been in Mrs. Carris' class nodded and recalled how much they had enjoyed the creepy story.

"Nice!" I said, "I didn't know teachers were using that story in elementary school. This week you're going to learn a lot more about Poe. We're going to start with this poem, and we'll get around to a couple others, like *"Annabel Lee"* and *"Alone."* Then we'll look at some of his short stories." Students shifted in their seats indifferently, and I handed out copies of the poem.

"Poe," I started, "was one of the most tragic writers in American literature. He was abandoned by his father when he was a baby, and then his mother died from tuberculosis when he was only about two years old."

"That sucks!" muttered a voice from the back of the room. I looked up and saw that it was Alex, one of my boys who rarely participated in class discussion. When our eyes met, he immediately looked down at his desk.

"You're right, Alex," I replied. "And it gets worse for him. He was taken in by his mother's friend, Frances Allan, but was separated from his older brother and baby sister. Francis' husband wanted his wife to be happy, but he didn't like Edgar right from the start."

"Did he abuse him?" Alex asked.

"That I don't really know. But he did send Edgar off to military school when he was old enough to go. Edgar added the name "Allan" to his name when Francis took him in, you see? Edgar *Allan* Poe?"

A few students "Oooooh-ed" as the concept of Poe's name came into focus.

"The story gets even more tragic for Edgar," I continued. "When he gets a little older, Francis died from tuberculosis, just like his mother had done." Several students gasped. "And with his adoptive mother gone, John Allen disowned Edgar, and kicked him out of their home."

"That's SO sad!" Madison, who was a bit dramatic, shouted.

"It is," I said. "And later on, Poe's wife, Virginia, also died from tuberculosis. She was only about twenty-five years old."

The class gasped audibly.

Madison raised her hand and asked, "Was he, like, a carrier? Did he have tuberculosis but just infected other people?"

"No, I don't think so," I said. There were a lot of tuberculosis going around at that time. Many people died. We're going to learn a lot more about Poe this week. He is famously thought of as the creator of the modern horror story. "*The Raven*" isn't all that terrifying, but it was his most famous poem."

"So, lets read it!" shouted Mariah, who often seemed bored with my lessons, but always seemed to soak everything in like a sponge.

"Good idea!" I replied. "But let's set the atmosphere a little bit." I let down the blinds and turned off the lights. There was still enough light in the room to see the text of the poem. Then I lit the candles and began to read as the students followed along.

"Once, upon a midnight dreary, while I pondered, weak and weary, over many a quaint and curious volume of forgotten lore..." "What's he doing?" I asked.

"He's reading an old book!" Mariah declared.

I tapped the raven, and it gave a loud reply. "Very good!" I said, "just doing some late-night reading!" I resumed reading the poem, *"While I nodded, nearly napping, suddenly there came a tapping, as of someone gently rapping, rapping at my chamber door."*

Now Madison piped up with, "So somebody is knocking at his door at midnight? I wouldn't answer it!"

"Smart girl!" said a boy's voice from the back of the room.

I stepped up to Madison, and as if I was answering her, I read on, *"'Tis some visitor,' I muttered, 'tapping at my chamber door. Only this, and nothing more.'"*

"I don't' care who it is," she said. "He better not open the door!" I leaned closer to Madison and gave the bird a tap, getting the desired nervous giggles from the students in the room.

I knew at that point that I had them hooked. They were getting into it. I read on.

"Ah, distinctly I remember, it was in the bleak December, and each separate dying ember wrought its ghost upon the floor. Eagerly I wished the morrow-- vainly I had sought

to borrow from my books surcease of sorrow, sorrow for the lost Lenore— for the rare and radiant maiden whom the angels name Lenore—Nameless here, forever more."

"Lenore is dead!" shouted another unidentified voice in the back.

"It doesn't say she's dead! It says she is nameless. What's that mean?" Alex had rejoined the conversation.

"He's sitting by the fireplace!" Mariah cried out. "He's watching the shadows of the flames and thinking about how sad he feels because Lenore is dead! Kyle is right!"

"I am?" Kyle looked surprised. I tapped the raven on the chest to acknowledge him.

"Well done, Kyle," I said. "You guys are doing great! Any questions so far?"

"Keep reading!" demanded Mariah.

"And the silken sad, uncertain rustling of each silken curtain thrilled me, filled me with fantastic terrors never felt before, so that now to still the beating of my heart, I stood repeating, 'Tis some visitor entreating entrance at my chamber door. This it is, and nothing more.'"

"So, wait," a new voice, that of Amanda, had joined in, "what does all that mean? He hasn't even answered his door and he sounds like he's more scared than he has ever been in his life."

"Yes, that's a good point," I replied. "Have any of you ever been right on the verge of falling asleep, and then, suddenly something stops you from nodding off? The phone rings, or the dog barks, or maybe somebody knocks at your door?"

Multiple voices responded, "Oh, I hate that!"

"Happens in my house all the time!" "My dog barks at everything that moves outside!"

"Your reaction is probably like the narrator of this poem. Suddenly you are awakened, and it shocks you so much that your heart is pounding, you're a little confused, maybe you even rose to your feet like this guy. I think he is so scared that he is imagining that the curtains are moving and he's just trying to get his bearings when he is telling himself that it's nothing but some late visitor at his door.

"That's cool, Mr. Sexton," Mariah said. "Can we go on now?"

I smiled and said, "Of course!"

"Presently my soul grew stronger, hesitating then no longer, 'Sir,' said I, 'or madam, truly your forgiveness I implore. But the fact is I was napping and so gently you came rapping, and so faintly you came tapping, tapping at my chamber door, that I scarce was sure I heard you'—here I opened wide the door—darkness there, and nothing more."

As I was reading this section of the poem, I walked dramatically to the door of my classroom, opened it, and peered into the hallway. Of course the lights were on, but when I turned and read the final line to the class, every face seemed to be gazing out the door as if expecting something to be there. I turned back to the open door, and resumed reading.

"Deep into that darkness peering, long I stood there wondering, fearing, doubting, dreaming dreams no mortal ever dared to dream before. But the silence was unbroken, and the stillness gave no token, and the only word there

spoken was the whispered word, 'Lenore?' This I whispered, and an echo murmured back the word, 'Lenore!' Merely this, and nothing more."

Madison, who had been hesitant about answering the door long ago, chirped up now. "So, this guy opened up the door and nobody is there, but some random voice said the name of his dead girlfriend? I'd be so out of there!"

A few students voiced their agreement and giggled nervously.

Mariah, never without an opinion, stated, "I think the guy is insane. He's just hearing voices, but they're in his head. He must be crazy."

Because the conversation was going so well without my intervention, I didn't comment. I continued to read the poem as the discussion tapered off.

"Back into the chamber turning, all my soul within me burning, soon again I heard a tapping somewhat louder than before. 'Surely,' said I, 'surely that is something at my window lattice. Let me see than what thereat is, and this mystery explore. Let my heart be still a moment, and this mystery explore—'Tis the wind, and nothing more.'"

"Wait," said Amanda, "so now he hears another tapping noise? Where is it coming from?"

"The window outside," replied Mariah.

"He's just imagining it. It's not real," Madison said, hopefully.

"It's Freddy Kruger!" shouted Alex. Several students laughed.

I tapped the raven to regain the attention of the class and continued to read.

"Open here I flung the shutter, when with many a flirt and flutter, in there stepped a stately raven of the saintly days of yore. Not the least obeisance made he, not a minute stopped or stayed he, but with mien of lord or lady, perched above my chamber door—perched upon a bust of Pallas, just above my chamber door, perched, and sat, and nothing more."

At this point, most of the faces in the classroom went blank. Finally, it was Alex who said, "So a raven came into his house? Or is he imagining he is at a palace? I don't get it."

Students nodded in agreement. Perhaps this was a little over their heads, but I tried to explain. "The narrator is saying that a raven came into his house through the window. I guess it flew across the room to the door where he had been standing earlier. He says it "perched upon a bust of Pallas." Pallas is another name for one of the Greek gods we studied a few weeks ago. Does anybody know which one?"

"Zeus?" asked Ryan, who had loved the unit of study on Greek mythology but had little interest in anything else we were doing in my Language Arts class.

"No, I think it's Athena, the goddess of wisdom and battle strategy. To tell you the truth, I don't know why Poe would have used a statue of her for the poem, but I bet he had a good reason."

"Mr. Sexton doesn't know something!" teased Amanda.

"No way!" I heard someone else shout.

I tapped the raven and went on with the next stanza.

"Then this ebony bird beguiling my sad fancy into smiling, by the grave and stern decorum of the countenance it wore, 'Though thy crest be shorn and shaven, thou,' I said, 'art sure no craven, ghastly grim and ancient raven wandering from the nightly shore—tell me what thy lordly name is on the nights Plutonian shore!' Quoth the raven, 'Nevermore.'"

"Is the raven named Nevermore? Or is he refusing to say what his name is?" Mariah asked.

"Maybe we'll figure that out as we keep reading, Mariah. Good question, though," I said.

Alex, surprisingly, was raising his hand from almost the very beginning of the stanza. Not waiting any longer to be called on, he asked, "Why was the guy smiling? I think I'd be scared if some big bird flew into my room. And what's "Plutonian shore" mean?"

"Wow!" I said, "Very nice, Alex. I think he's not seeing the raven as a scary thing at this point. It's just a harmless bird; perhaps somebody's pet. It randomly flew into his house and now it's almost like a guest, or a visitor. Like Mariah said, maybe it even has a name. The "Plutonian shore" is meant to make it creepy. Poe is referencing the god of the underworld from Roman mythology, Pluto. He's kind of implying that the raven came from a place of death."

"Cool," Alex sighed, impressed.

"So, I know this is a really long poem, but let's see where things go next," I said.

"Much I marvelled this ungainly fowl to hear discourse so plainly, though its answer little meaning—little relevancy bore. For we cannot help agreeing that

no living human being ever yet was blessed with seeing bird above his chamber door—Bird, or beast upon the sculptured bust above his chamber door, with such name as "Nevermore."'

"I knew that was its name!" Maria declared proudly.

"But the Raven, sitting lonely on that placid bust, spoke only that one word, as if his soul in that one word he did outpour. Nothing farther then he uttered—not a feather then he fluttered—Til I scarcely more than muttered, 'Other friends have flown before—on the morrow he will leave me, as my Hopes have flown before.' Then the bird said, 'Nevermore.'"

"This is creepy," Madison chirped, nervously.

"Why do you say that?" I asked.

"So, this bird flies into his room and sits on a statue and says, 'Nevermore,' then it stands still? It doesn't even move a feather? I think this guy is crazy or something."

"That's interesting, Madison. A lot of people thought Poe was crazy when he wrote it. Some people thought the character he created as the narrator was meant to sound like he was crazy. Poe would go on tour, reciting his poem to audiences. He got to be very well-known for it. Sometimes little children would chase him down the street and he'd turn around and flap his overcoat like a bird and yell, 'Nevermore!' at them. They loved it."

There was a pause as the students digested the idea of Poe playing in the street with children.

I tapped the bird and said, "Let's see what happens next."

"Startled at the stillness broken by reply so aptly spoken. 'Doubtless,' said I, 'What it utters is its only stock and store. Caught from some unhappy master, whom some unmerciful Disaster followed fast and followed faster, till his songs one burden bore—till the dirges of his hope that melancholy bore, of 'Never—nevermore'!"

"Madison raised her hand but didn't wait to be called on, "What does "stock and store" mean?" she asked.

"Well," I replied, look at the context of the sentence, Madison. The narrator says, "What it *utter*s is its only stock and store." To utter is to speak, right? So, what do you think he means?"

"That 'nevermore' is the only thing the raven can say?"

"Exactly! Well done, Madison," A few students gave Madison some playful applause, and I noticed she was smiling proudly.

"So how did the bird learn to say 'nevermore?' Alex asked.

"The narrator says the raven had 'some unhappy master,' in the stanza we just read. Maybe he taught it to speak. What happened to the unhappy master?"

Alex studied the stanza for a moment and said, "He died?"

"Maybe. There was an 'unmercial disaster' of some kind, right?"

As the class fell silent again, I decided this was a good time to resume the poem.

"But the raven still beguiling my sad fancy into smiling,

straight I wheeled a cushioned seat in front of bird and bust and door. Then upon the velvet sinking I betook myself to linking fancy unto fancy, thinking what this ominous bird of yore—what this grim, ungainly, ghastly, gaunt and ominous bird of yore, meant in croaking 'Nevermore!'"

"Ugh!" Kyle rejoined the conversation, "I'm lost! What's he talking about? I mean, I understand that he wants to know what the raven meant by 'nevermore,' but what's all that other junk about 'fancy unto fancy?' Several students grumbled in agreement.

"You're right, Kyle. He's trying to figure out what the bird means, and he is making connections… thinking it over. So, the Raven has the narrator's attention when the narrator grabs a chair and sits down in front of it," I explained.

"Oh, like a captain's chair, because it has wheels?"

I looked at the text again and said, "Oh, I guess so. I didn't see that until you mentioned it."

"Good catch, Kyle!" A random, male voice spoke up in the dimmed classroom. I didn't recognize who it was, but there seemed to be a hint of sarcasm in the voice.

A pause followed, so I started back on the poem.

"This I sat engaged in guessing, but no syllable expressing to the fowl whose fiery eyes now burned into my bosom's core; This and more I sat divining, with my head at ease reclining on the cushion's velvet lining that the lamp-light gloated o'er, but whose velvet-violet lining with the lamplight gloating o'er, She shall press, ah, nevermore!"

(As I read, I ignored that unidentified voice that

had chimed in with "He said 'bosom!'" and laughed like Bevis and Butthead.)

"Oh! Oh! I get it!" Mariah showed up to save the day. "The cushion! The cushion that he's sitting on! He is saying that Lenore, the girl who died, won't ever sit on that cushion again! She used to sit against that same cushion that he is sitting on, and now he's realizing that she never will again!"

"Cuz she's dead," the voice in the back of the room spoke more audibly now, but nobody reacted to him.

"Really good, Mariah!" I said, peering into the unlit corner in the back of the room, and seeing nothing.

"Then, methought, the air grew denser, perfumed from an unseen censer Swung by seraphim whose foot-falls tinkled on the tufted floor. 'Wretch,' I cried, "thy God hath lent thee—by these angels he hath sent thee respite— respite and nepenthe from thy memories of Lenore; Quaff, oh, quaff this kind nepenthe and forget this lost Lenore!' Quoth the Raven, 'Nevermore.'"

The crickets suddenly chirping along with the sound of students' breathing let me know I had lost them. Not a syllable was expressed by them or by me for a full thirty seconds.

"What's a seraphim?" Alex asked, finally.

"Yeah," I said, "there are several words in that section that you don't typically hear in your daily conversations. I meant to give you some of them in vocabulary before reading this, but I got so excited to read the poem with you that I forgot. Seraphim are angels of the highest order in heaven. Some stories say the Seraphim are the angels that protect God himself. The narrator is sensing a presence in the room and saying that's what it must be. But then he uses some other words that are confusing to the average student. He calls the Raven a "wretch," which is an insult. But what I kind of find troubling is that he is suggesting that God sent the Raven to his home. Yet the Raven is a thing of evil, so it almost seems like the Raven is a punishment."

"For what?" Alex again.

"For killing Lenore!" the unidentified voice spoke up more loudly this time.

None of the students reacted to the voice or turned around to look where it had come from, so I took a step or two in his general direction. I still couldn't find him, but I thought his answer was interesting, and I repeated, "For killing Lenore? Maybe."

"That's sick!" Madison squealed.

"We don't know if he did that or not. There are a couple more words we should discuss too. He mentions 'respite and Nepenthe.' Nepenthe was a drug used in Poe's time to help someone forget things. It was to fight off depression. So, the narrator is saying he hopes to get 'respite,' or rest, by quaffing some Nepenthe. Quaffing means to swallow. So the narrator is asking if he will ever be able to forget the pain of Lenore's death, and what does the Raven tell him?

"Nevermore!" two thirds of the class responded loudly.

"'Prophet!' said I, 'Thing of evil! Prophet still, if bird of devil! Whether tempter sent or whether tempest tossed thee here ashore, desolate, yet all undaunted, on this desert *land enchanted—on this home by horror haunted—tell me truly, I implore—is there—is there balm in Gilead? Tell me—tell me—I implore.' Quoth the Raven, 'Nevermore.'"*

This time several students joined me in saying "nevermore," and I could tell they were having fun with the poem.

"So, I know you're not going to know exactly what he means by 'balm in Gilead,' right?" Nobody replied, but I thought I again heard that voice in the back of the room, this time it was repeating what I said as I explained the meaning. It's hard to hear what someone else is saying when I am talking, but as I stumbled over my words, it almost sounded like the student in the back was actually saying them *before* I was! Weird! "He is asking if there is anything he can do to get relief from his grief and haunted memories of Lenore. He wants to escape his pain. And what does the Raven say about that?"

"Nevermore!" all the voices in the class seemed to shout it out this time, but the one that stood out was the one in the back. The pitch had grown higher than a normal voice, and angry. I walked to the back of the room where the voice had come from, glanced around, and resumed the poem.

"'Prophet!' said I, 'thing of evil! Prophet still, if bird or devil! By that Heaven that bends above us—by that God we both adore—tell this soul with sorrow laden if, within the distant Aidenn, it shall clasp a sainted maiden whom the angels name Lenore—clasp a rare and radiant maiden whom the angels name Lenore.' Quoth the Raven, 'Nevermore.'"

"At this point in the story, the narrator is saying that the Raven is something evil." I looked around the room, searching, "But he wants it to tell him something. Does anybody know what it is?" Nobody seemed to know, and the mysterious voice was silent. "Let me give you a little help. He asks the Raven to tell him if Lenore is in 'Aidenn,' which is an Arabic word for Eden, or maybe, Heaven."

"So, he wants to know if Lenore is in Heaven?" Mariah asked.

"That's right, Mariah. He wants to know if the woman who he loved, the woman who died, made it into Heaven. And what does the Raven say?"

"Nevermore!" I heard the unidentified voice, only now it was on the side of the room I had moved away from! I hadn't seen anybody get up all this time, yet I distinctly heard that angry, abrasive voice.

"That's terrible, Mr. Sexton!" shouted Madison. "Not only did the love of his life die, but she didn't even get into Heaven. That means…"

"She's in Hell!" said the voice, now seeming to come from everywhere.

My eyes swept the classroom. I knew I needed to continue with the lesson, but I was starting to feel quite uncomfortable, as if the air had suddenly grown dense. I went on with the poem again.

"'Be that word our sign of parting, bird or fiend!' I shrieked, upstarting— 'Get thee back into the tempest and the Night's Plutonian shore! Leave no black plume as a token of that lie thy soul hath spoken! Leave my loneliness unbroken! Quit the bust above my door! Take thy beak from out my heart, and take thy form from off my door!'

Quoth the Raven, "Nevermore."'

"My favorite line of the poem is in that stanza," I said, "Can you guess which line it is?" When nobody replied, I said dramatically, *"Take thy beak from out my heart, and take thy form from off my door!"*

"Did the Raven stab him in the heart with his beak?" Ryan asked urgently.

"No, it's a figure of speech," I explained. "Being told that your loved one is not in heaven is as if someone stabbed you in the heart, isn't it? That's how he feels."

"And he's kicking the Raven out because it made him so mad, right?" Alex added.

"Good, Alex," I replied, "he tells it to get back out in the tempest, or storm, outside. Don't even leave a plume, or feather, as evidence of the lie you just told about Lenore. When the Raven says, 'Nevermore' again, it seems to be refusing to leave!"

"I'd get my shotgun and blast that raven," said Alex.

"Kill him!" said the mysterious voice.

"Final stanza," I announced. "Let me know what you think when we finish, but please raise your hands because I think you guys are going to have some awesome things to say and I want everyone else to be able to hear you."

Students nodded, and I read the last stanza.

"And the Raven, never flitting, still is sitting, still is sitting on the pallid bust of Pallas just above my chamber door. And his eyes have all the seeming of a demon's that is dreaming, and the lamp-light o'er him streaming throws his shadow on the floor. And my soul from out that shadow

that lies floating on the floor shall be lifted—nevermore!"

Several hands went up, but I called on Mariah because she had been following so closely throughout the reading and had made several excellent observations.

"I think the person who is narrating the poem is actually Edgar Allan Poe," she said.

"Really? Why do you say that Mariah?"

"Well, you said that all these people in his life died, just like Lenore died. So, I think the poem is about losing the people in your life that you care about and how depressing it is when that kind of thing happens. My dad died when I was only seven, but it still hurts, and I think it always will," she sighed deeply, and I felt a lump emerge in my throat. "Poe is saying that when someone you love dies, the pain of the loss will always be there." Mariah paused and I could see the pain she still carried in her face. "Well, that's what I think."

"Wow," I said. "A plus, Mariah. You said that beautifully. I guess the Raven is a symbol of the pain you're talking about. No matter how hard you try, you can never make the pain go away."

Mariah nodded solemnly.

There were other comments in the class that followed Mariah's, but none so brilliant. I let students discuss the poem among themselves for the last few minutes of class. I blew out the candles and turned the lights back on. I searched around for the strange voice among the students in the class but didn't find it. I knew that it would be back again in the next class, and the next, and the next. And the voice from in that classroom shall remain there, Evermore.

-Fin-

BIO

Randy Sexton was born in 1957 in Los Angeles and raised in multiple Southern California cities from Los Angeles to San Diego. He attended elementary, junior high, and high school in South Pasadena until the middle of his eleventh-grade year. Then he was brutally torn from the womb of this comfortable life and thrown into James Madison High School, in San Diego. This school was two hours south of South Pasadena. This was a fine school, but there were twice as many students as South Pasadena High School had. Unfortunately, not a single one could be called a friend.

At the age of nineteen, Sexton moved out of his parents' home and into a three- bedroom apartment in Fullerton. Two old friends were already living there, and the addition of a third roommate made the rent much easier for them. He lived with these friends for almost two years, but when they decided to move their girl-friends into the apartment, all Hell broke loose.

Sexton had spent these years working in the kitchen of a hospital and attending Mt. San Antonio Junior College, where he got a small taste of college life.

A wild hair caused him to move to Fairbanks, Alaska, in search of a high-paying job working on the pipeline. That job never came, but he managed to find good-paying, short term jobs in construction and also worked in the back of a refrigerated truck carving up fresh salmon for same-day shipment around the world.

After spending the summer in Fairbanks, he moved to Kentucky, where his parents now lived. Here he attended the Universities of Kentucky and Louisville and worked in psychiatric hospitals and group homes so he could afford to pay his tuition. He earned his bachelor's degree in English, along with a teaching credential in English for grades 7-12.

During this time, he also co-directed a summer camp for at-risk youth and, along with several counselors, took these young people camping at places around southern Kentucky and even to the Appalachian Trail on the Georgia and North Carolina border. It was this experience that first opened his eyes to the fun of working with young people who are out of their element (sort of like the first time they are in a middle school building).

Five years passed before Sexton moved back to California, this time with his new wife, Jackie. Their son, Tyler, was born in 1993. Sexton worked at the private *Jack Weaver School* at the Oak Grove Institute, in Mur-

rieta. This was a residential treatment facility for adolescents who had been removed from their homes for
engaging in dangerous and sometimes life-risking behaviors, including gang violence, criminal behavior, and
drug use.

A job here required a degree in the field of Special Education, so he attended the University of California at Riverside and got his master's degree. He spent six
years teaching some incredibly challenging students at
this school but enjoying the rewards that came when he
could help guide the students to successful completion of
their programs.

Randy. Jackie. And Tyler returned to Kentucky
so he could accept a public-school teaching position in
Melungeon County, which is not the real name of the
county but is used to preserve the privacy of the actual
location. Back in Kentucky, Sexton completed a second
master's degree from the University of the Cumberlands
as a Reading Specialist.

Sexton retired from teaching in 2017. He and Jackie
enjoy cruises to Caribbean destinations. They do volun-
teer work with organizations such as Mentors and Meals
(a middle school enrichment program) and Kentucky
Great Dane Rescue.

They now live in Versailles, Kentucky with their
rescues, Odysseus-Kane (pictured on the cover), and
Hera. They entertain thoughts of moving to St. Peters-
burg, Florida, whenever the writing career provides the
necessary funds.

COMING SOON!

Randy Sexton is currently working on a second book that co-mingles narrative stories with lessons teaching young people about the plays of William Shakespeare, poetry writing techniques, and great works of literature including Greek mythology. These lessons include his own transcript of the plays, instructional techniques, and assignments for students. They are fun for adults too! The stories will be written much like the story that appeared in this book, "Why You Got That Bird For?"

Made in the USA
Middletown, DE
26 September 2023

39475156R00066